Amongst the Aliens
Some aspects of a gay life

Peter Burton was born in 1945 and has spent thirty-five years between publishing, bookselling and journalism. He has written for a wide range of newspapers and magazines and written, co-authored or contributed to more than thirty books – including *Rod Stewart: A life on the Town: Parallel Lives; Talking to . . .; The Art of Gay Love; The Boy From Beirut; Vale of Tears: A problem shared* and *Drag: A history of female impersonation in the performing arts.*

Francis King is the author of almost forty books, including *A Domestic Animal; Voices in an Empty Room; The Ant Colony; The One and Only; E M Forster and his World* and *Yesterday Came Suddenly*, an autobiography.

Richard Smith is a freelance journalist. Publications he has written for include *Gay Times, The Guardian, Melody Maker* and *MixMag.* He is co-author of *Drag: A history of female impersonation in the performing arts* and is currently working on a book about homosexuality and popular music for Cassell.

D1206366

Amongst the Aliens
Some aspects of a gay life

Peter Burton

Foreword by Francis King
Afterword by Richard Smith

Millivres Books
Brighton

Published in 1995 by Millivres Books (Publishers)
33 Bristol Gardens, Brighton BN2 5JR, East Sussex, England

Amongst the Aliens: Some aspects of a gay life
Copyright (C) Peter Burton, 1995
Foreword Copyright (C) Francis King, 1995
Afterword Copyright (C) Richard Smith, 1995
The moral rights of the authors have been asserted

A CIP catalogue record for this book is available from the British Library

ISBN 1 873741 21 9

Typeset by Hailsham Typesetting Services, 4-5 Wentworth House,
George Street, Hailsham, East Sussex BN27 1AD

Printed and bound by Biddles Ltd., Walnut Tree House, Woodbridge
Park, Guildford, Surrey GU1 1DA

Distributed in the United Kingdom and Western Europe by Turnaround
Distribution Co-Op Ltd., 27 Horsell Road, London N5 1XL

Distributed in the United States of America by InBook, 140 Commerce
Street, East Haven, Connecticut 06512, USA

Distributed in Australia by Stilone Pty Ltd, PO Box 155, Broadway, NSW
2007, Australia.

For

Pam and John, Mr and Mrs Tubby Bear

and

Michael and Matthew, the cubs

and

The February cats, Ben, Joe and Ruby

Contents

Foreword .... Francis King
In the Beginning 3
Whoops! A sad gay racket 5
Girls on the Gay Scene 9
Sing a Gay Song: Some aspects of gay rock 17
On the Shelf: *The Rush Before the End* 27
Blind Dates? 31
Don't Say That 39
On Being Bashed 43
Christmas Comes 49
Growing Up Gay, Going Grey 53
Too Much of a Good Thing 57
Dressing Up 63
Middle-Aged Spread: A riposte 69
Jealousy 75
The Cottaging Taboo 79
David Bowie: The man who invented himself 87
Great Expectations 93
Rock Hudson: The full story? 97
Across the Great Divide 103
Andy Warhol Looks a Scream 109
He's So Fine 113
Amongst the Aliens 119
Men in the Kitchen 123
Is It Really Pink? 127
Who Does the Dishes? 131
The Enemy Within 135
Coping With the End 139
The Prospect of Rotterdam 148
Sappho at the Stove 155
Playing Up 161
The Way We Wore 165
Sweet Dreams 169
Subversives 173
Teen Idols: `Are you or have you ever...?' 179
New Kids on the Block 183
Remembering Denis 191
Afterword .... Richard Smith

FOREWORD

There are half-a-dozen or so literary pages which, because of the combined enthusiasm, knowledge and shrewdness of their editors, contrive to exert an influence out of all proportion to the smallness and narrowness of the readerships of the periodicals in which they appear. In particular, I am thinking of Matthew Lewin's book pages in the *Ham and High*, Isabel Quigley's in the *Tablet*, and Mark Amory's in the *Spectator*. I am also thinking of Peter Burton's books pages first in *Gay News*, long since defunct, and now in *Gay Times*. Whether I should continue to read the last of these magazines were it not for its arts and literature sections, I rather doubt.

Peter Burton was already very much part of the gay scene at our first encounter, at least twenty years ago, when he was acting as indispensable adviser, amanuensis and friend to the novelist Robin Maugham. But his interests have always extended beyond that scene, and therein lies his strength both as a writer and as a literary editor. Inevitably writings by homosexuals and concerned with homosexual themes have demanded much of his attention. But, in conversation, I am always amazed by the breadth of his reading, and by his ability to analyse, appreciate and even become enthusiastic about works as straight as a Roman road.

It is this catholicity which makes this volume into something of more universal appeal than its subtitle 'Some aspects of a gay life' might suggest. One of my favourite essays is 'On Being Bashed'. The bashing is a queer one, suffered by Burton himself in Brighton, where he has made his home; but much of what he writes about the experience is equally applicable to a bashing of any kind in the increasingly violent society in which we now live. 'I still keep thinking about it *and wondering if it will happen again*'. Every victim of a bashing, whether homosexual or heterosexual, has wondered the same thing. The destruction of the victim's confidence in the world around him is usually far more pernicious in its long-term effects

1

than any physical injury.

Again, the entertaining essay on dating-services and the mordant on jealousy, though treated from the homosexual viewpoint, have much to say that will be of interest to the heterosexual as well; and 'Coping with the End', a moving account of Burton's loss of a friend to Aids, will have an agonising relevance for all those, no matter what their sexual orientation, who have been faced with the early death of a loved one.

Other essays which I particularly enjoyed were an amusing disquisition on Fifties styles in male dress; an affectionate and touching tribute to Denis Lemon, editor of *Gay News*, rightly described by Burton as 'a man of immense charm, caustic wit, shining intelligence and great entrepreneurial skill'; and an attempt to reach some understanding of that most enigmatic of pop stars David Bowie. This last is a reminder that, at one time, Burton worked in the entourage of Rod Stewart, about whom he has written a vivid study.

Throughout this volume, as he deals with subjects as diverse as gay rock, the approach of middle age, class distinction, the pink pound and Rock Hudson's secret life in a Hollywood in which no star could admit to being homosexual, Burton is always lively, always provocative, always stimulating, always humane.

He is the ideal spokesman, at once forthright and balanced, for the homosexual community.

Francis King

IN THE BEGINNING

My first published journalism appeared in the *Walthamstow Express and Independent* in 1962. My journalistic career proper began in 1965, when I was asked to write for *The Stage* (to which I still occasionally contribute). My career as a gay journalist commenced in 1968 – with the second issue of John D Stamford's *Spartacus* – and took flight the following year when I became first theatre critic and then a features writer and subsequently editor of *Jeremy*. I haven't looked back . . .

The articles reproduced in *Amongst the Aliens: Some aspects of a gay life* range across twenty-five years of contributions to the British gay press and reflect both my attitudes and opinions and aspects of British gay history over that time. Obviously these pieces are but the tip of an iceberg of words I have written about gay culture and gay life. I hope they have a flavour . . .

The pieces vary in length – mainly because the confines of space in newspapers and magazines usually dictates the length to which a journalist can write – but I have resisted the temptation to re-write, revise or expand for fear of causing distortion. The articles also appear in the sequence of original publication – in the hope that they will build a picture which, perhaps inevitably, ends with Aids and loss. This is not to suggest that Aids is an inevitability of gay life. Far from it. Loss, however, is an inevitability of life – one of the few sensations all humanity must share.

There are large numbers of people whom deserve acknowledgement for the help and encouragement they gave me at various stages of my life: Roger Baker, Doris and George Burton, Michael Davidson, Eric Johns, Kris Kirk, Denis Lemon, Raymond Marriott, E C Mason, Robin Maugham, Ian McGee and David Rees (all of whom need the prefix 'the late' before their names); Chris Graham-Bell, Billy Gaff, Mike Gill, Peter Hepple, Michael Lowrie, Joe McCrindle, Colin Spencer and many others (still living).

For particular assistance, encouragement or support during the preparation of this book, I must especially thank Sebastian Beaumont, Francis King, Simon Lovat, Richard Smith and Michael Tomkins.

WHOOPS! A SAD GAY RACKET

The Boys in the Band has been running in London now for a year, for even longer in New York, and we are shortly to be treated to a film version of it. The play has had the dubious distinction of being issued complete on a set of long playing records. And that *is* unusual; *Who's Afraid of Virginia Woolf?* is one of the few other modern and recent plays to have been issued in this way. Charles Dyer's *Staircase*, though not issued as a record, has been as fortunate as *Boys*. The play came first, staged by the Royal Shakespeare Company and starring Paul Schofield, one of Britain's leading actors; then two of the screen's biggest stars, Burton and Rex Harrison, made the much condemned movie. And the *Staircase* success story doesn't stop there either. Author playwright Dyer did his own screenplay too, then dug out all his old notes and ideas for the original play project, worked them over – we're told the notes ran to something near a thousand pages, and produced a whacking great novel of the play of the film. So it goes on. And, oh yes, almost forgotten, the script of *Boys* is available in book form too. *Cherry, Larry, Sandy, Doris, Jean, Paul*, by Jack Larson played a short season in London in the summer, when the University of Southern California Drama Division brought it over with them. Colin Spencer's domestic comedy, *Spitting Image*, had a wildly successful run at the small Hampstead Theatre Club a year ago and later transferred to the Duke of Yorks. Landford Wilson's *The Madness of Lady Bright*, seen at the International Theatre Club over a year ago, was well received by the liberal press, but was given only a limited run and not half the acclaim it should have received.

Each of the five plays mentioned has one thing in common. Each of them is concerned, in some way or other, with homosexuals and homosexuality. The first two were wildly successful, the other three definitely weren't. Why?

Well, let's go back a bit and look at some other plays that have used this box office potential theme. Way back, when most of us weren't even thought of, London and New York saw a play called *The Green Bay Tree* (Mordaunt Sharp, London 1933, with Frank Vosper, later to die in rather mysterious circumstances). The plot concerned an elderly gentleman, assuredly a disciple of Saint Oscar, and his young ward. The run was good, and the play, still an amusing period piece, achieved a certain notoriety because of it's theme of corruption of a young man by an elder. It ended with a delicate scene with one combing the hair of the other: not very daring for today, but it certainly made people talk then. It would be interesting to see how well this play would go if revived now; it certainly couldn't be worse than some of the plays we see in London. Funnily enough, a direct descendant of *The Green Bay Tree* did make an appearance in the West End about five years back – Pauline MacCaully's *The Creeper* which sported that excellent actor Eric Portman as a bizarre elderly gentleman with a liking, implied rather than openly stated, for young men. Naturally it had one or two tricks up on *The Green Bay Tree*, but it wasn't all that far removed, and the stink of corruption and decay hovered over the entire stage household: something sinister in the bed.

For a while the New Watergate Theatre Club had a run of plays with a decidedly homosexual interest. The Lord Chamberlain wouldn't grant a licence for public performance to plays like *Cat on a Hot Tin Roof*, *Tea and Sympathy* or *A View from the Bridge*. His reasoning was pretty wonky in each of these cases, for in the first the alcoholic sportsman hero wards off his repressed homosexuality; in the second a schoolmistress offers herself to save a boy she thinks is queer, and in the third the embrace between two men which the censor objected to wasn't a sexual kiss at all but one between two jealous heterosexual men, one of whom was trying to imply the other was queer. Yet in the last few years the number of plays with a real homosexual theme has escalated alarmingly. Even small experimental theatres have presented plays which contained an almost statutory gay character. Some of the plays have been good like *The Killing of Sister George*, some bad like the brutal and unconvincing *Fortune and Men's Eyes*. *Fortune and Men's Eyes* had such a success here, and a good critical reception, that it's been revived in New York by actor Sal Mineo, and even sexed up some. The previously off-stage rape now takes place, so the American reviews announce, bang in front of the audience, simulated, of course, not the real thing. Actors have yet to manage erections on stage, and who'd care to give eight public performances of that kind every week? Even the most hardened exhibitionists would find it a bit of a strain.

But back to our main theme, those five plays mentioned earlier – the whys and wherefores of their respective successes and failures. *Cherry, Larry, Sandy*, reviewed in the first issue of *Jeremy*, was written, for some eccentric reason, in verse. But the play had massive charm and miraculous compassion. *Cherry* followed the course of events between a gay affair and their travelling companion girlfriend. The very use of a girl in this situation represented a real step forward in homosexual writing and the fact that the boys were written about as normal boys made a change too.

The Madness of Lady Bright is probably one of the best representations ever seen on stage of the decline of a gay man. The central character is written about with real feeling and real understanding, is not sensationalised or depressionalised and the picture we get is sympathetic. The only laughter is with the character not at him.

Colin Spencer's *Spitting Image* is in a slightly different category. For this play,though it started out in a small club, was obviously destined for bigger things from the beginning. The main situation in this comedy was that boys were physically capable of becoming pregnant, and the ending of the piece, pure farce, had militant homosexual mothers and fathers storming a centre to rescue their progeny from the hands of mad scientists. The scorn heaped on this production from some quarters showed a frightening loathing of homosexuals still strongly exists, but despite vicious reviews the play has gone to New York, and is to be made, some time in 1970, into a movie. In each of these three plays the gay characters

7

have been represented as human beings, with feelings, fears and desires, shown as men, not mincing monsters out of a McGill comic postcard.

But *Staircase* and *The Boys In The Band* showed the other side of the coin: the unpleasant outrageous picture of homosexuality that is good for a fast buck because it is acceptable to press and public alike. Why? Because the homosexuals in both plays are of the lisping, mincing, perfume-reeking, mother-ridden kind. *Boys* is the most offensive in this respect and it is a pretty poorly written play on top of that. Isn't it basically two one act plays, one comedy and one drama, tied together to make a full length piece? It may be that things are very different in the States : maybe the queer scene is all closely knit, without allowances for youth or life, concerned with nothing further than the latest petty drama, and lacking women. For it is certainly true in this country that the younger crowd is becoming more of a bisexual crowd. Here we no longer get so much misogynistic spoutings. But *Staircase* and *Boys In The Band* have proved successful and *Fortune and Men's Eyes*, viciously anti-queer, was also a success in a limited way. They prove that the subject does have box office potential: when it is dressed in the way the public want it dressed: when the men, or women, represented are shown as the public have always thought of or imagined them – lisping, flapping their wrists, effeminate – and UNNATURAL. As the posters for the film of *Staircase* cry : "Whoops! a sad gay story". And that's just about it. The attitudes of the theatre towards homosexuals is a sad gay story and is likely to remain so until more plays like *Lady Bright* and *Spitting Image* are given a fair chance. Until then we'll get homosexuals on stage, but they'll only last if they're like the other misfits, the petty crooks, the drug-addicts – who are even more maligned and ignored – because they're 'poor sick things' to feel liberal and sorry for. Not to think of as natural, normal men worthy of respect and attention. Just to feel sorry for. It really is a sad gay story.

JEREMY January 1970

GIRLS ON THE GAY SCENE

Ten years ago in London, and no doubt too, outside the capital, it was a rare sight to see a girl or woman in a gay club or bar. And if any female was in one she had to be pretty brave and thick-skinned to override the hostility directed at her. Women – a decade ago – in those specialised circles – were just not welcome.

Things have changed a lot, however, and these days the situation is completely reversed, though there are still a few last strongholds of homophile masculine society. A lot of this change must be put down to the Youth Revolution, which has affected sex, homo and hetero, strongly, vigorously and healthily. These days sex isn't an exclusive province, for either boys and girls, girls and girls, or boys and boys, or men, but something general, something to be enjoyed for its own sake and not because of any previously, rigidly, imposed sociological or psychological reasons.

These days if there weren't girls on the gay scene it would seem pretty strange. They've finally broken in – some think for the better, some for the worse – to this last exclusive "club". Below are interviews with two girls who've been on the London scene for some time, one since she was fourteen and one since she was seventeen. Iris is nearly twenty one. She was born in, and still lives in, Bethnal Green. She's small, about five foot, slightly dumpy, always casually dressed, and a very definite original. It's hard to tell what the years will do to her but there's a strong chance that, if she carries on the way she does, she'll make it as a genuine London character. Her overwhelming characteristic is her cockney exuberance and her sense of fun, yet to talk to her is to discover a depth of sensitivity and understanding the casual on-looker, or acquaintance, would not expect.

"I was going out with this boy, we were engaged. Then he went into prison and I went out with a girlfriend of mine and discovered I had lesbian tendencies.

"A friend came up from Stevenage and took us all to *The*

Discotheque, which was open a few years ago, and then, when all those clubs shut down, someone said, "There's a nice new queer club down here", but it wasn't new, we'd only just discovered it. So we all went, Tommy included, who at the time I didn't know was queer. So we all went down there and there was such a nice atmosphere, and we loved it, that I stopped taking lots of pills . . . I used to take hundreds of pills before, when I was about seventeen, but when I started going to the gay clubs, I stopped taking them, because I didn't need them so much, the people were so nice and friendly, I thought.

"Then this girlfriend of mine, Jane, not a lesbian girlfriend, just a friend, she used to be madly in love with Tommy, who's the sort of boy next door I grew up with and love passionately, and she used to say to me, "He's going off with a man, he's going off with a man." And I'd say, "No he's not. Don't be silly. He's normal." I wouldn't believe it. After we'd been down there a couple of weeks, The *LeDuce*, I got to know a few people. All the boys were saying, "He is queer" and I was saying, "He's not, he's not." But I knew all the time that he was.

"Then one day he said, "I'm going to Morden with this boy, that one with the white bumpers I told you fancies me." I didn't believe it. I had this imaginary pigeon on me shoulder" – (she chuckles) – "I used to have fantasies about pigeons – and I was walking along the street talking to me shoulder. Because I couldn't believe he was going off with a boy . . . and I thought I had a pigeon there and was saying to it, "He's going, he's gone and left me." And he went. And I didn't know what was going on because he went with two girls and this boy, Bill, who wasn't a queen, but he was camp in a way. He had short hair and white bumpers and big ears. So he went and when he came back Tommy kept saying, "I've got something to tell you." For weeks. Every time I asked him what it was he'd say, "No. I'll tell you tomorrow." Then one day I decided he must tell me that he was gay, cos I knew that was what he had to tell me, but I wanted him to tell me himself. So I took him on a bus and I gave him some pills. We were going to Morden, to see his boyfriend . . . fucking big ears. We got on the bus and I gave him these drugs and I was saying to him, "You're not gay are you Tommy?" and he was saying, "No, of course not." "You would tell me if you was?" "Yeah, course I would," he said. When we got there I thought: 'This is going too far'. And there were these other two girls, one of whom was supposed to be going out with fucking Big-Ears and was pregnant at the time, having screaming dramas over Tommy, which I didn't know about – cos I wasn't supposed to know that he was gay.

"I just happened to mention that some boy had said he'd been to bed with Tommy, and Tommy said, "Iris. Come here, quickly." And he told me. And I said, "That's all right, I knew." But when I went back into the other room I burst into tears. I was horrified at the thought of it. I couldn't believe it and I cried for six weeks at the thought of it. Now when I look back I think I must have been silly because it's better for him like that.

"I couldn't bring myself to come to terms with him for about two years after that. He went with this boy for seven months, lived with him, and they had dramas and things and I witnessed them. But I became quite friendly with this boy, Bill, and I still am friendly with him and one day I might marry him . . . cos he's quite nice really and he hasn't got big ears, well, he has but . . .

"Then a boy I knew from the "Scene Club", another normal club, came down. He was sort of rather beautiful and I'd once had a mad crush on him for about a week . . . but I hadn't seen him for a year. He came down with his ex-girlfriend. We were sitting in the restaurant upstairs. His name was Roger. We were sitting in the restaurant with this boy Stevie, who was a waiter there, and I had my arms round Roger and he was playing with Roger's neck. And Roger was horrified at the thought of being touched by a man. Then I went for a long walk with him and he said, "I want to go back to that place." He liked it. So I found out another one of my close friends was queer. I thought: When is it going to stop? Two of my closest friends queer.

11

"So I really am involved in it . . . I can't just stop going on the gay scene, it's not just for the fun of it. Roger's not like he used to be now, and Tommy's away at sea . . .

"I've been on the gay scene for three years now and I think I've come to terms with it. Sometimes I think I'm queer and sometimes I think I'm not. I do fancy girls occasionally; but I wouldn't go with them. Although I have been with one or two in the past, but that was long before I was ever on the gay scene.

"The people on the scene are all very young or they're all old, there's no inbetween . . . they're all either very, very young and have been going for about six months or a year and think they know it all, think they're beautiful, but after a year they suddenly go to pieces . . . after having various affairs, v.d. etc . . . find they're spotty and aged and can't cope. Then there's the older ones who've been around for six to ten years. Some of them are a bit piss elegant, cos they think nobody can know what it's like unless they've been around as long as they have. A lot of these older boys don't like the girls . . . they think they interfere.

"I like some of the young people who go to the *LeDuce*, I go there a lot, and *Yours or Mine* . . . I don't like *Yours or Mine* because it's full of grotesque trying-to-look-young pretentious beings. Whenever I go there I feel out of place . . . I come from the East End and they all seem to have money. If you haven't got something new on every week, you know, they talk about you and if one of your hairs is out of place they're all whispering about it. I like *LeDuce* now, but it got a bit bad there last year. I sometimes go to the gay pubs. I don't really like the *Boltons* and *The Pink Sisters*.

"The girls on the gay scene? Some of them are okay, but only the ones that have been on it for a long time. Most of the younger ones think that the boys are queer but that they haven't "Met me yet", and think they can turn them normal. They're queer and that's the way they like it. That's why I said that when I look back on it, about Tommy, I'm glad that he's gay. Because I'd have lost him otherwise, to another girl, and I think I would have disliked that more than to a boy.

"I suppose I'll grow up one day, cos I don't really think I'm grown up although I'm twenty, nearly twenty one. I suppose one day I'll stop doing all this but I don't know when, can't see it coming, perhaps I'll kill myself. I don't think anybody grows up on the gay scene . . . at all . . . whether they're a boy or a girl. They never grow up.

"I don't like the slagging, the way people slag each other on the gay scene. Although I do quite a bit of it myself. And I don't like people who scheme, though I do that as well. But you have to. To survive. Otherwise they'd crush you into the ground. I suppose I'm a bit of a bully with some of the gay boys, because I know I can push them around more than I could the normal ones.

"I don't like normal boys at all. I've gotta brother . . . and whenever I bring queens home he just . . . my mum likes queens, but he doesn't. Even though Tommy who was my close friend was his close friend for just as many years as he's been mine. We all grew up together. He just says, "Well Tommy's different." But he's not different at all. He won't realise this. This is what the point is about normals. I don't like them at all. I once brought some gay people home on a Sunday morning. And this boy who's rather bold sat there holding one of my brother's friends, who's supposedly normal, holding his hand and groping him. In front of my mum. She didn't like it very much at all, she didn't mind gay boys kissing, but when it came to a gay boy touching up my brother's friends, she didn't seem so keen. She forbade the boy to come ever again to the house and my brother said that he'd beat him up. But it wasn't really fair, because the other boy was entirely agreeable to what they were doing, and even took the boy to the door and kissed him goodbye. When I asked him about it I said, "Are you queer, Alan?" He said, "No, I just wanted to try it out . . . "

"This is a load of old cock if you ask me . . . nearly every boy must be gay. They must have a little bit of it in them . . . most of them. And that's why they don't like it."

✳ ✳ ✳ ✳ ✳

13

Ann is twenty two, was born in the East End, but lives now, with her parents, on the edge of Ashdown Forest. She is of medium height, about five six, tends to be a bit overweight, but it suits her, rarely dresses casually. She is usually seen in something stark and startling, in an outfit to make heads turn. It's difficult to tell, with her as with Iris, what the years will do. Her slightly odd family background might mean that she's carrying on a kind of tradition and will suddenly settle down and marry one of her gay boys. Though it doesn't seem very likely. She doesn't come over as the marrying type.

"I first got onto the gay scene when I was about fourteen. I had a Saturday job in a local poodle parlour and the two girls who ran it were both dikes. They used to take me out with them, to Earls Court and clubs like *The Place*. My dad's queer anyway and I never needed to be told that my older brother was gay. I just knew it. Female intuition if you like. But going around with dikes and mixing with queers anyway, I didn't need to be told.

"Then when I stopped going to the poodle parlour I started to go around a bit with my brother and his boyfriend. We used to go to some really horrific clubs. Once I was sitting on my brother's lap and actually got told off for it. But there were some blokes down there practically having it off in the corners. Maybe they thought I was a transvestite or something. In those days there weren't many girls on the scene and the reaction to them was always a bit peculiar. I've often found myself the only girl in one of the drinking clubs.

"Really it's quite nice having a camp dad; most of my friends who know him say he's a laugh, and me and my brother tell everyone about him. He's kind of a seventh wonder of the gay world. People are always asking us how he is and when friends of mine ring up he's always chatting them up and inviting them over for dinner.

"At one time I used to go out with a lot of normal boys but now I only go to the gay pubs and clubs. I much prefer the company of gay boys, they're so much more polite and more fun, and at least you know that if they take you out

14

it's because they like you and not just to get their hand up your skirt. Not that that's even true these days. Everyone seems to be experimenting and there aren't many of the younger gay boys, those under twentyfive, who've not been with at least one girl. Mind you, it's ever so easy to get off with gay boys.

"There aren't any good clubs to go to now. The ones that are open are either too piss elegant or are so grotty that it's an embarrassment to be seen going into them. There doesn't seem to be any happy medium. It really is time someone opened a good new club up, cheap, pleasant and inexpensive.

"I've never had and Lesbian experience, though I did mix with Lesbians when I had my Saturday job. Never fancied it at all, they always seem so bloody aggressive. The ones you get around the West End certainly are. I've had quite a few affairs with gay boys but you have to realise that you can't turn them normal. I lived with this boy John, everyone used to call him Samantha, who looked more like a girl than me. Except that he didn't have tits. He used to wear most of my clothes, blouses and things. I thought I was in love with him at the time but when I look back on it now it really embarrasses me. Especially if people talk about it to me. They must have all thought I was an absolute fool. Mind you I was only a "gay young thing" at the time.

"Then I had this thing about a junkie queen, and that was only last year, but I put that down to a brainstorm on my part. He's in a right state now and we all expect him to die at any minute.

"The girls on the scene nowadays are such a scatty lot. I'm sure half of them don't even realise the boys are queer. At least you can say that the older girls have a certain amount of style. But it's all changed. Once the girls were there as rather glamorous ornaments. To dress up and preen. To make an entrance with. Now girls are just girls. Most of them seem right little scrubbers – I sometimes seem to be one of the few left who bothers to dress up at all. But all these silly little things at the clubs now . . .

round and round in circles for the first person who pays them a bit of attention. They all think everywhere's so good. They don't know how good it all used to be.

"Where do I go? Oh, *LeDuce*, *The Union*. I even once went to one of those grope-arama cinemas with some friends. And when the lights went up everyone was trying to work out if I was some big drag number.

"I go around with this darling little boy now. He's only seventeen and everyone thinks that we're knocking it off. But we're not. I'm like a mum to him, and wouldn't like to see him get into trouble. I enjoy his company and he always looks so nice. Not scruffy like a lot of people. That's the trouble with my brother he always looks as if he's fallen off the back of a corporation dustcart. We have a funny sort of relationship. In a way we're much more friendly than most brothers and sisters but we don't mix with the same crowd too much. These days I go to the clubs and that more than he does. But then he's getting old, he's twentyfive, and probably thinks it's time to retire gracefully.

"I'm one of the oldest girls on the scene. None of them seem to stay around after twenty two or three. God knows what happens to them. They can't all commit suicide and I'm sure they don't get married. Maybe they just become cranky old women somewhere. I can't imagine what's going to happen . . . I'm almost too old for all this now and the kids on the scene get younger and younger all the time. It's nothing to be in the West End these days at fourteen. And when I was fourteen twenty two seemed ancient. It's different for the boys, this is their natural habitat . . . but what about the girls when they get older. You always hear boys saying "Get that old geezer over there" but do you ever hear them saying, "Get that old bird over there, she must be fifty if she's a day"?"

JEREMY May 1970

SING A GAY SONG
Some aspects of gay rock

We never did find out what "Me and Julio" were up to by
the old schoolyard. We were a bit surprised when Ian
Matthews sang "Do Doo Ron Ron (when he walked me
home)." We had our suspicions about what the "Something
Strange" was which Peter Frampton, in the old Herd days,
sang about. We all knew about "Lola", but she was a pretty
exceptional case. Most of the time we've been left guessing.

Guessing about what?

Gay rock, that's what. Where is it?

And the term gay rock is used in this context to cover
any kind of gay popular music.

For those who like to read, it's easy enough to pop down
to the friendly neighbourhood bookstore (even W.H.
Smiths) and find a novel or polemic volume of homosexual
interest. It's not that desperately difficult to find either a
play or a movie with some kind of strong gay appeal –
after all, even if the production is obvious, anti, or over
camp, the talking point is still there. For those of us with an
interest in painting – well, David Hockney and all his
lovely young men spring instantly to mind. But there's
plenty of art of a homophile nature. Even gay ballets have
started to make a strong showing. Classical music?
Tchaikovsky is a good, if obvious, example. It's a fairly well
accepted thesis that Tchaikovsky wouldn't have composed
the way he did had it not been for his homosexuality.

But where are the exponents of gay rock? They seem to
be so thin on the ground that they are well nigh invisible.
Certainly it's difficult to think of a recording British gay
rock artist.

What about David Bowie? most people will say. Not
really. He's a very different case. Fine, so Bowie came out.
But he's hardly writing gay rock songs. Other than "Queen
Bitch" how many other overtly gay Bowie songs can you
think of?

But that's just Great Britain.

America, on the other hand, is an entirely different cup of noodles.

In front of me, as the typewriter clatters away, are seven American gay albums. Six of them are on small, independent labels. One of them is on a major label – the first gay album (excluding the comedy album *God Save The Queens*) to have been issued by a major record company. These albums vary in quality and content. They range from polemical and boring, to romantic, to downright, honest, raunchy homosexual rock and roll. But, in a strange way, the contents don't matter. For the simple fact that these albums exist is what is important. Exist they do. But they exist only in America. As far as it is possible to ascertain, none of them are likely to get either British release or distribution. So unless you have contacts in America, or are a jet-setter, it's going to be fairly difficult to come by copies of any of them.

Of the seven albums (there may well be more, if there are they haven't come my way), two have a wide appeal. The other five have somewhat restricted horizons. It is these five we will examine first.

Michael Cohen used to be (may well still be) a New York taxi driver. His first album appeared under the title *Mike Cohen* and was released in 1973. The record label is a bit difficult to work out; but it seems to be Diadelphous Stamens Inc. A Not For Profit Corporation. Cohen has written all of the songs on the album, and the material ranges from somewhat convoluted and difficult lyrics heavy with homosexual awareness to classically simple lyrics which, at their best, remind one of the early Paul Simon.

The most notable song on the album is called "Ward Six (Special Care Unit)" which was inspired by a short story by Chekhov. The lyrics are simple, clear and have a haunting pain about them:

> *With sunken eyes that hide the scar*
> *his madness takes him very far*
> *he drifts where lovers learn to weep*

18

he lands where darkness covers sleep
and children sleep
and cry for water in the night
O in the night . . .
And like my messengers of old
he rides his stallion in the cold
I saw him breathe his fiery breath
I saw him leave the house of death
while I was starving
for salvation or a sign
O just a sign . . .

So the song continues through two further subtle verses. The strength of the song lies in the allusion as opposed to the obviously stated. It is a fine piece of craftsmanship (strangely reminding me, in places, of some Oscar Wilde poem) which would fit well onto any album – be it homosexual or heterosexual. In Mike Cohen's case, it is his subversive songs which are the most persuasive. As homosexuals, we have to live with heterosexual art, in this instance heterosexual rock. There is no reason why homosexual rock should not as easily clutter the airwaves. But it is the subversive which is the most beguiling. A hint of something unknown – as in the previously mentioned "Something Strange" – is infinitely more captivating than the obviously political.

Mike Cohen has been lucky. Obviously his first album found its way into the attention of those with power to do something about it. For following the first, a second appeared. This time the packaging was slicker, more professional. Most important, Michael Cohen's *What Did you Expect?* appeared on a small, but distinguished, label: Folkways Records.

What Did You Expect? is some of the best from *Mike Cohen* and some new material. Strangely, "Ward Six" is not on this new album, but, as with the first, the best songs are the simplest, the ones which insidiously worm their way into consciousness. Of this the best two examples are "Couldn't Do Without" and "Bittersweet" (based on a

Leonard Cohen poem).

Lavender Country originates out of Seattle, and is distributed by Gay Community Social Services of Seattle. This community has been involved in a counselling service, community centre, gender identity clinic, VD clinic, and has provided extensive resources in community education through speaking engagements and symposia. In 1973, one of the major undertakings of the community was the amassing of financial resources for the *Lavender Country* album.

The album strikes me as very much country and western orientated; and as such it has, for this country, a double limited appeal. For if someone is going to consider putting out a gay album here it is unlikely that they would consider a gay country album.

In my notes on this album is this comment: "Too political for it ever to have the chance of moving beyond the confines of the initiated."

Obviously gay activism has been, still is, of immense value. Especially in America where it is helping to evolve an awareness of gay culture (awful expression, but unavoidable). But . . . and it is a BIG but . . . the heavily homosexual material always seems as oppressive as oppressive propaganda by anti-gays. Lyrically *Lavender Country* shows, to my personal taste, too much awareness and not enough art. It's easy to appreciate what the community have put into the album, but appreciation doesn't excuse the boredom the album induced.

Eric Bentley's *The Queen Of 42nd Street* only just slips into this collection of albums – slips in by one song, the title track of the album. Bentley is better known as a theatre critic, as one of the major translators of Brecht, and as author of such books as *The Theatre Of Commitment*.

The Queen of 42nd Street is a collection of Jaques Prevert's poems with a musical setting by Joseph Kosma. In the original French version, "The Queen . . . " was about a woman, but on the album, in this translation, Bentley has turned the woman into a gay guy, and set the whole in New York, where he has performed the song at dinner clubs.

20

"The Queen Of 42nd Street" has a lot in common with Bowie's "Queen Bitch". She (and this is a good instance of using a switch in gender identity legitimately) is tacky, a bleached blonde, aging, dressed far to gaudily, in fact, an obvious queen. But the song she sings is life affirming, she doesn't care. She's happy and that's all that matters.

This is the way I am. Yes, I'm just made this way
And when I want to laugh, why then, I laugh all day
I dig the guy that digs me, so how am I to blame
If the guy that digs me is not every night the same?
Well, that's the way I am, I'm made this way you see
And what more do you want? What do you want from me?

Bentley's delivery is sub-Coward, and Kosma's music has a nicely decadent Thirties feel to it. If only for this one song, *The Queen of 42nd Street* is an album well worth trying to get.

The final album in this batch is almost completely romantic. Paul Wagner sings gentle love songs with titles such as "But I love", "I Don't Know", "Need Your Love Too" and "Meadows of Peace". This album, *To Be a Man*, has a different feel about it. It doesn't hector, it doesn't make any promises, doesn't make any claims, isn't there to make any great statements. The message in this album comes across simply because it doesn't try: simply because the songs are romantic and gentle.

However, of the albums written about above, it would be difficult to honestly say that any one of them is totally entertaining, totally enjoyable, worth spending hard earned pennies on. Each has interest if you're especially interested in what is happening by way of gay rock music. Outside that the pleasures are there, but mainly they are small pleasures, one or two songs per album, maybe only stray lyrics.

Steven Grossman and Chris Robison have both produced albums which do have a great deal to offer, albums which are well worth collecting.

Both Grossman and Robison are New York boys. Both

have written New York albums with a definite sense of that most exciting of cities about them.

Steven Grossman has the distinction of being the first self-confessed homosexual rock artist to have a homosexual album released by a major record company, Mercury (a label Grossman shares with Rod Stewart). Moreover on this album, *Caravan Tonight*, Grossman seems to be aiming only for a gay audience. He isn't in the least concerned about the heterosexual who may have an interest, may simply have read a review and purchased. For the ungay, lines like:

> *And I don't want to go down on my knees and elbows*
> *And not have you do the same – the same*

would be fairly difficult to follow. Or would they? Is it simply a naive assumption that straight people don't know what gay people do in bed? They *must* have a pretty good idea.

Caravan Tonight is obviously an autobiographical album. Steven Grossman is writing about what he knows and what he has experienced. "Out", for example, is a clever little song about telling parents and family of gayness. The punch is in the fact that the word gay isn't used until the very last line, though words for gay are suggested at the blank ends of each verse. "Circle Nine Times" is about one of the best of the Greenwich Village gay bars, the Ninth Circle. But Grossman has his personal hang-ups and in this song he is explaining that:

> *There's something that still isn't right*
> *All this boozing and cruising does nothing more*
> *Than to give me the pain in my song*

Though Steven Grossman has accepted his homosexuality, he hasn't accepted a lot of the problems, personal emotional problems, which seem to be part of his being homosexual. (Is that remark asking for trouble? But let it stand.)

He's not happy about promiscuity, but he is aware that it

exists, and his awareness pushes him in the direction of further understanding. Both "Circle Nine Times" and "Dry Dock Dreaming" are about casual sex. "Dry Dock Dreaming" is about the truck-parking area down by New York's East River. Gays congregate at these empty and unlocked trucks – the area known as The Trucks – for instant sex and, incidentally, all too frequent muggings. (Anyone who watched *The Detective* on television recently will recognise The Trucks in the long and aggressive riverside frisking scene). Grossman understands instant sex as a product of loneliness.

> *Oh Lord won't you help me, I'm tired and stoned*
> *I'm anxious and angry and want to go home*
> *But not all alone*

Possibly this album works so well, lyrically particularly, because it is so autobiographical. Throughout – even on the less good tracks – there is a painful honesty. Grossman is confiding his problems to us, he is sharing his excitements and discoveries. There is no happy ending to *Caravan Tonight*; the final track is "Dry Dock Dreaming" and the ultimate lines are far from happy.

> *Well what I do to your body I can do to your head*
> *Oh do to your head – well, come on mister let's do it again*
> *Oh Devil won't you leave me I'm turning to stone*
> *I'm anxious and angry and want to go home*
> *But please not alone.*

But knowing you're capable of fucking someone's head is going a long way to understanding why you shouldn't do it. And he who fucks heads always runs the risk of fucking his own.

Chris Robison's album *Chris Robison and His Many Hand Band*, is completely unlike any of the other albums written about in this piece. In many respects all of the others want to explain, want people to understand a point of view, want understanding. Chris Robison doesn't ask anything.

His album is there. And that's it. There really aren't any messages about it – except "Go with the flow; enjoy what you are."

Even more than Steven Grossman, Chris Robison has written a New York album; possibly the definitive New York gay album. He has captured the speed, the hang-ups, the feeling of anticipation which seems to hover like a dust cloud over New York. His lyrics are powerful, often touchingly beautiful. His music ranges from raunchy honest-to-God rock, through gentle melody, to a sheer sing-along anthem.

Track one, Side two: "I'm Looking For A Boy Tonight" is probably the most direct and straightforward gay song yet written:

> *I'm looking for a boy tonite*
> *I know to some of you out there*
> *it may not seem quite right*
> *But I am not the only one*
> *to know your own sex can be fun*
> *That's why I'm looking for a boy tonight*

is the chorus verse, and it says it better than anyone else has managed.

It is the sense of sheer pleasure in his homosexuality which makes Chris Robison so unique. He doesn't appear – on record at least – to have any problems. Creatively, Chris has achieved a nirvana-like state of complete acceptance of himself and if anyone is shocked, well, he seems to say, they don't know what they're missing.

More than anything *Chris Robison* is a sexual album. There is a romantic air about most of it but when Chris sings

> *Feel the love all around you*
> *And every day will astound you*
> *Ride your rainbow through the air*
> *And you will find your castle there.*

it is glaringly apparent that at the end of that rainbow

24

that's a bloody good fuck.

And surely – isn't that what it's all *really* about? It's all very nice to think in non-sexual terms, but sex is fun. All those boy/girl/moon/June songs are really about boys and girls getting it together. Why shouldn't there be *joyous* celebration of gay guys and gay girls getting it on and enjoying it? That's what Chris Robison is writing about.

Enjoying being homosexual.

All of the others, it now strikes me, don't seem to have much fun.

Chris has the good fortune to be beautiful and talented and good copy; he's received a fair amount of press, most of it good, in America. Not just in gay publications either, he's been favourably noticed in everything from *Cashbox* (the leading American music trade magazine) to *Rolling Stone*.

Chris has a second album ready for release; *Manchild*. He says of it that "It has been in the works for over a year. In it's music and words I try to paint an *overall* picture of what it's like to grow up, to deal with love, sex, boredom, death, sadness, and elation." It should be worth waiting for.

But why are there no British gay albums? Why are there no likely releases for any of the albums discussed above?

Surely it is no more risky for Phonogram to release *Caravan Tonight* than it was for Elektra to release (and hype like crazy) the Jobriath album. It's a pity we can have Chris Robison on Elephant's Memorys' *Angels Forever*, and not have the individual and unique solo album.

Obviously British record companies feel there is no demand for gay rock, and that the demand there may be is not worth considering. Of course, the ludicrous airplay situation with the BBC must contribute to an unwillingness to put money into anything that is unlikely to get into the BBC's top thirty formula playlist.

Legality may have something to do with it. For America hasn't had a change in law; homosexuality is still against the law in most states. Yet under an atmosphere of theoretical legal oppression gay culture flourishes (clubs and bars are a damn sight better Stateside, too). Here the change in the law has helped to bring about a hoped-for

25

integration. Somewhere up there, amongst Our Betters, there is someone saying:

"Gay rock? What's that? And who wants it? We've changed the Law. What more do they want?"

It is interesting to consider – If the law had not been changed, if we were still all committing a crime each time we clambered into bed with another man or boy, would there be a set of gay singer/songwriters writing and recording in this country?

It seems highly likely.

GAY NEWS August 1975

ON THE SHELF:
THE RUSH BEFORE THE END

In the late 1950's and the early 1960's, Royston Ellis was touted as the English 'King of the Beats'. He was a youthful prophet of the Bomb-generation – author of several collections of poems, of which *Jiving to Gyp* was the most notable, a slim volume on *The Big Beat Scene*, and a novel called *Myself and Fame* which detailed the rise of a pop singer. This latter book was made memorable by a neat comic scene in which the hero awakens in his manager's bed. He wonders why his bum is sore. On looking over the side of the bed and observing an open jar of Vaseline, he realises why. The scene seemed to go very far – for that was back in the early Sixties.

A lesser known novel by Ellis, *The Rush At The End* (Tandem Books, 1967) is well worth reconsidering, for it touches on themes which are too often ignored in gay novels, or if not ignored, treated superficially – encroaching old age and incest.

The hero of *The Rush Before The End* is Arthur Darby, a senior clerk in a London office. He is a few years short of retirement and seems contented in his commuter rut. The name Darby (as in Darby and Joan) seems to have been carefully chosen. Arthur is married, with a placid wife, Amy, and a grown-up daughter who lives away from home. His life couldn't appear more ordinary and dull.

At the beginning of the book Arthur goes into the toilet at Waterloo – he has lunched too well and urgently needs to pee. He has a disquieting experience – for the young man in the stall next to him makes sexual advances. Arthur ignores the youth and hurries away to catch his train. His usual compartment is full and Arthur has to stand for most of the journey home. But seated in the carriage is a boy of about twenty whose appearance attracts Arthur – he is clean cut (Arthur cannot stand "those Teddy Boys") and personable. Arthur begins to remember incidents in his past, with youths, and these give him an erection. He considers this due to too much liquor at lunchtime.

Ellis then gives a detailed (and rather cruel) description of Darby's home, wife and home-life – typically suburban, centred around instant food and television. Suddenly Arthur sees how boring his existence is. The following morning he gets up early and hopes that he will see the clean-cut youth again.

Eventually, of course, Arthur does meet the boy (Andrew) and they strike up a grudging train journey relationship. Andrew is a college graduate, working in a London office and sharing a small flat in Epsom with an old school friend. The relationship between Andrew and Chris, the school friend, is intense and it is obvious that they are having an unacknowledged homosexual affair. Yet Chris is predominantly heterosexual – and when he dates girls, Andrew feels left out and jealous. At a party with Chris and his current girlfriend, Andrew drops acid (LSD) and 'freaks out'. He also encounters a bizarre and heavily drugged girl who does a striptease.

Meanwhile the relationship with Arthur is developing. Andrew is invited back to Arthur's home. To make things appear more 'natural' Arthur also invites his daughter, Jane. Neither Jane – the archetypal 'drop out' – nor Andrew are much looking forward to the evening. But Jane turns out to be the girl who did the strip at the party at which Andrew was tripping. To Arthur's suppressed jealousy, Andrew and Jane hit it off immediately.

It is from this point that the novel becomes really interesting. For Ellis now intertwines his relationships – Andrew loves Chris, but Chris gets married, Andrew turns to Arthur for comfort but Jane also falls for Andrew. The only person who really gets left out is Arthur's sweet but ineffectual wife – not only is she left out, she simply doesn't notice what is going on around her.

Arthur becomes totally obsessed with Andrew. Yet to keep up pretences he often invites Jane along on outings with Andrew. This means that though he is aware there is a strong physical attraction between Jane and Andrew – and though he feels he must protect his image – he has to use the daughter of whom he is jealous as cover. Jane, needless to say has had lesbian experiences and realises what Daddy is up to. But she doesn't mind. In fact at one point she asks Andrew what Daddy is like in bed, she's always wondered and has always rather fancied him! Jane represents liberated living – drugs, drink, sex: "That's part of the liberation of the younger generation which we keep on hearing about. No inhibitions over sex. All for all and all for all. Girls, goats, queens, queers, even men. No prejudice. Sexual integration." she tells Andrew who has yet to be liberated. Later in the same chapter Jane looks 'across at the sleeping BSc (Andrew) beside her and thought that he had a lot to learn. But she could see what her father saw in him.'

Running counter to the sexual revolution which is being fought throughout *The Rush At The End* is a theme which follows Arthur's elevation to the Board of Directors of the firm he works for. The two themes meet when Arthur takes Andrew to Majorca for a brief holiday. One night in a gay bar they meet the one Director of the company who has seemed opposed to Arthur's being made a Director. But as soon as he realises that Arthur, like himself, is gay the position changes.

Arthur returns to England to find that Amy has tarted herself and the home up. But Arthur considers that Andrew is more important to him. He gives up home, job and all his old conceptions of life. As the novel ends Amy is going to open a tea shop, Jane is heavy with Andrew's child, and Arthur and Andrew are about to return to Majorca to open a beach bar.

The Rush At The End is most definitely not a great novel; it is hardly even a good one. Yet it has some special quality which makes it memorable. It is certainly an honest book which takes a cool look at the peculiar sexual traumas which *may* affect a middle-aged man when marriage has staled and life has become drearily predictable. Arthur is a well-drawn character, his emotions and responses are completely believable – and Ellis is at pains to stress that Arthur's homosexuality isn't some startling new development, rather the flowering of something he has suppressed throughout his life.

Andrew and Jane work less well – it is difficult to imagine someone with the apparent sex appeal of Andrew totally throwing in his lot with someone like Arthur. And Jane really is too much to be true; she is one of those awful pre-hippy hippies whose ideals are admirable but who, in cold print, becomes positively unbearable.

Unfortunately Royston Ellis wrote *The Rush At The End* in the jargon of the period: the era – and how long ago it now seems – when London was 'swinging'. Nothing dates faster than slang and the use of expressions like 'Square gear', 'With It', 'In Crowd', 'What a buzz', 'That's Wild' etc. date the book horribly. In fact the whole ambience Ellis so lovingly creates now seems so distant in time as to be historic (maybe we're about due for a revival of plastic mini-skirts and hipster trousers).

Yet for its many faults *The Rush At The End* is enjoyable and strangely memorable. Presumably written as a pot-boiler, the book remains well-intentioned and takes a far more realistic look at a section of the gay world than many of the more seriously written novels of the period. Ellis may not be the greatest writer in the world – and he has rather sunk from view over the last few years – but *The Rush At The End* is a novel with its heart in the right place. Even more remarkably, considering the date it was written, it has a happy ending – maybe not for the straight characters, but certainly for the gays.

GAY NEWS May 1977

BLIND DATES?

What does the idea of a dating service – heterosexual *or* homosexual – suggest to many people? Usually the image conjured by a non-member of a dating service, about a member or prospective member, is of someone who has given up all hope of personally meeting or making contact with another individual in the sexual or emotional marketplace. This individual is imagined as being no longer desirable – but perhaps they never were; almost certainly no longer young – whatever that most doubtful of words may mean to each individual taste. To be a little more concise, most people have an ingrained suspicion about dating services because they believe that it is only life's failures who use them.

But are these beliefs and doubts justified? If we are to believe Bill Glenn (of Adam International), Emma Read and Mel Laroche (who runs GAYWAY), or Jason Renolds and Nick Ferrier (of MALE-LINE), these suppositions are completely wrong – a set of attributes which should have been thrown out with the baby's bath water.

Though it is easy enough to find companies which offer introductions, it is probably Adam International, GAYWAY and MALE-LINE which have attracted the attention of *Gay News* readers – not least because all three services take large display advertisements in the pages of the paper. Obviously, therefore, the people to question about same-sex pairing were those best qualified to know – the five people who run the three companies mentioned above.

Bill Glenn, who heads Adam International's compact organisation – and is assisted by David Young – is middle-aged, avuncular, with the easy charm and a dash of the manner of a Noel Coward hero. From a tiny office above London's Regent Street – cluttered, overcrowded, and seemingly endlessly busy – Bill directs an operation which claims members as far afield as Saudi Arabia and the United States of America. Adam International, unlike either GAYWAY or MALE-LINE, offers more than one

31

direct service – and though the backbone of the company is the gay introductions, the organisation also handles flat-share accommodation, an escort service, counselling, group therapy, a box number service, and is currently trying to organise monthly social events at which members can meet each other on a more personal and informal basis.

Emma Read and Mel Laroche are more high-powered – at least, Emma is. She bubbles over with all the enthusiasm of Dolly Levi (the match-making heroine of *Hello Dolly!*), talks a lot – each sentence punctuated by "Do you know what I mean?" – and is obviously intensely committed to her job. Mel is her lover – and a direct contrast; quiet, almost shy – but with a delicious winning smile. GAYWAY, of the three companies the one which is the most widely known, is strictly a dating service – though members are offered a wide range of discounts from other gay businesses (sadly, almost exclusively London based) on production of their membership card.

Jason Renolds and Nick Ferrier are comparative newcomers as far as running a gay dating service goes – although both directors of MALE-LINE have experience of them as members. Far more anonymous than Bill Glenn or Emma and Mel, Jason – who is in his mid-thirties, and Nick – fortyish? declined to have their photographs printed with this article because they felt it could be enormously embarrassing for members to come face to face in a club or bar with the 'cupids' who had arranged their dates (although Jason's silhouette does grace the company stationery). At the moment, MALE-LINE handles neither other concerns nor offers incentives to join – the sole aim of the company is to focus complete attention on the introductions. Jason and Nick feel that dating services are much needed (a sentiment shared by Emma and Mel, and by Bill Glenn) and incline toward the view of 'the more the merrier' – "Gay people have got another dating or introduction service", said Jason. "There was one, there were two. Now there's three. There could well be more; who knows. At least they've got a choice."

Though each of the dating services here under discussion has the same essential aims, all three of the companies present a slightly different image. The first obvious difference a prospective member will notice is in the advertising – Adam International (who used to be Adam Bureau, but changed their name because of the marked increase in overseas membership) use fairly straight-forward, almost sombre advertising; GAYWAY's promotions are more splashy and noticeable and, in *Gay News*, at least, appear to change from issue to issue; the advertising for MALE-LINE is fairly simple – but with an appealingly humorous touch to it.

The second noticeable difference is in whom the adver-tisements are aimed at – for both Adam International and MALE-LINE are geared towards male-to-male introductions, while GAYWAY aim towards male-to-male and female-to-female introductions. Though providing a service for both gay men *and* women, Emma pointed out that GAYWAY membership is about " . . . seventy per cent male and thirty per cent female". Jason and Nick stated that they are not undertaking introductions between gay women because " . . . as males, we feel that we are not mentally or biologically qualified to match up the opposite sex."

Each dating service sends prospective members a brochure cum application form which outlines the aims of the company. When the form is completed and returned, along with the required membership fee (with Adam International this is £20 for five introductions; GAYWAY is £14 for five dates; MALE-LINE is £15 for "up to six intro-ductions"), this is processed – and the speed with which the newly signed member gets their first dates appears to depend upon two major factors: availability of a compat-ible date; and the workload which is currently being processed by the service joined. Bill Glenn reckons turn-around time, from acceptance of membership to first date, is "usually within two weeks", though he adds the proviso that if the member's requirements are difficult to fulfil, he will notify them that it will take a little longer. Both GAYWAY and MALE-LINE thought two weeks was about the average time, too, between acceptance and first date –

but Emma was quick to point out that there have been happy instances when new members have been able to receive their first introduction "by return of post".

Emma and Mel, Nick and Jason, and Bill all stressed the high confidentiality of the service they provide – the records are kept locked away; in one instance a duplicate set of records is kept in a bank vault; and security is high. The degree of information this kind of service necessitates is of a very personal nature – and each of the companies is well aware that it could be disastrous if their records were lost or fell into the wrong hands.

"We have always encouraged honest and straightforward personality profiles from members, about themselves and the sort of person they are looking for, and our Interests Page, though quite detailed, is an integrated part of the membership application, because all members enclose an additional letter as well as an up-to-date clear facial photograph, which is for our use only", Emma expounded. "People are quite happy to do this, and we do not work without one, because we must have the face to put to the name, the person we are going to get into, get to know, and deal with. Naturally, many people are anxious that such intimate details about themselves do not fall into the wrong hands, and we have a watertight security system for the safety of our members, who do come from all walks of life . . . plumbers, teachers, doctors, guards, executives, producers, actors, storemen . . . up and down the social scale."

And how is the actual introduction arranged? Is there an impersonal and unfeeling computer lurking in each of these services' offices? Far from it Bill, Emma and Mel, and Jason and Nick, all stressed that each of set of introductions is carefully worked out and selected by themselves – it is all personal, not a computer in sight; fallibility is possible – but, at least, that fallibility is human. Hours are long, too – for again, each individual stressed that they wee dealing with delicate human emotions; something that cannot be messed around with nor treated simply as a means to make a fast buck.

Who joins a gay dating service? And why?

"There's no one type", says Bill Glenn. "We get a lot of people who are tired of the 'scene', fed up with one night stands, people who have simply heard about us, people who are a little bit shy, people who are out of London and have no local clubs or bars to frequent, people who would rather leave the whole thing to an expert. I actually encourage people to come in for a personal interview – fifty percent of our London members do that – and out-of-towners are encouraged to come and see us when they are in London. Members range up and down the age scale from twenty-one to seventy, but I'd say the bulk of our members are between thirty and forty – that's definitely where the bulge is. And I do believe that there's someone for everyone. We don't take anyone on unless we can help. If we do feel that someone is unhelpable we let them go, we return their cheque . . . and perhaps we will recommend them to a gay counselling/befriending service, such as Friend, say . . . "

Is the stigma attached to dating services breaking down, then? Emma Read certainly thinks so.

"Undoubtedly, one of the hardest things to achieve, on an overall balance, and one that has certainly taken years to accomplish, has been to break the social stigma often attached to dating services", Emma explained. "1978 saw the biggest changes in the types of clients Gayway attracted, but '79 has seen the biggest changes in our membership as a whole, and we are going into the Eighties with an extremely attractive and up-market young membership, because word has travelled that Gayway can be a great way and a fun way of meeting new people, and, above all, that our membership does not consist of social outcasts. In fact, quite the reverse. Sex certainly isn't a problem for the typical Gayway member, and we have some stunning looking people on our books, as well as the more ordinary type of person."

Jason Renolds and Nick Ferrier tended to agree with Emma's point of view – though their comments were a bit more cautious.

"Our youngest member is twenty-one", Jason said, "the

eldest is sixty-five. But the bulk of our membership comes from the twenty-five to thirty-eight age group."

Nick picked up the conversation at this point."There *is* a certain amount of stigma attached to them," he explained, "but I think that may be because dating services are something which doesn't get a lot of recommendation by word of mouth. For example, both of us have been members of dating services and though we've been close friends for about fifteen years now, neither of us told the other about it – until one night when we were both a bit pissed. There is a stigma, I think – but it's going.

"Eighty percent of our members ask for everything to come under plain cover", Jason resumed, "which we do as a matter of course. Everything is marked 'Private and Confidential'. But yes, there is a stigma. It *is* beginning to disappear, but it won't disappear completely for a long time."

Emma Read has been running GAYWAY for five years; Bill Glenn has been running Adam International for nearly three and a half years; Jason and Nick started MALE LINE just over three months ago. They all admit that the hours are long, the work draining – if emotionally rewarding. But why start a gay dating service in the first place?

Bill Glenn feels that there is a tremendous need for this kind of service and went on to say that he enjoyed "helping people to become more themselves."

"Gays have had a choice of pubs, clubs, hotels, holidays, various services, magazines in which to advertise," Jason said, "so why shouldn't we have a choice in the field of dating services?"

"It's our aim to direct our combined efforts towards reducing the large number of lonely and isolated gays," Nick added. "We want to provide a genuine and honest service through which compatible gays can meet."

"Though adjusted to being gay, I was totally rejected by my family, for my sexuality", Emma told me, "and this realization of rejection and what it might mean to thousands of others, combined with a genuine fascination with people and what makes them tick, provided me with the incentive and determination to provide a progressive and longterm service for gay people to meet interesting and new friends."

So do gay dating services work? It looks as if they might.

In the five years of their existence, GAYWAY have handled over eight thousand memberships – and have a constantly changing clientele which totals about three thousand five hundred at any given time. Both Bill Glenn and Jason and Nick spoke about the steady increase in the number of members they attract.

It is interesting to contemplate why there is a need for gay dating services – even more interesting to consider that London, Great Britain's leading gay metropolis, holds a large number of the gay dating services' members. Are people genuinely becoming tired of the gay 'scene' – it would seem unlikely, especially as it is ever expanding. Or do gay dating services fulfil a greater need? Offer something which cruising clubs and bars simply do not offer? Or is it simply something as basic as we are all different – we all want different things – and we all go about finding them in different ways?

GAY NEWS Feb 1980

DON'T SAY THAT

Language changes: new words evolve, old words subtly or substantially change their meaning, political or sexual trends may make some words dangerous to use and others thoughtlessly discriminatory. However, just sometimes it seems that the changing language is not being enriched – unless one considers verbal boobytraps a form of enrichment.

Words change – but people's use of those words rarely change as quickly and this can give a whole new complexion and complication to 'speaking the language like a native'.

Some years ago we were having Sunday lunch with my parents – my sister and a gay boy friend, my lover and myself. Ian was suffering from a heavy cold and as Steven, my sister's friend, was about to sit down next to him on the sofa my father suggested: "I shouldn't sit next to Ian. He's a bit queer."

We all shrieked with laughter – and my father had the good grace to realize that he'd used a rather inappropriate word. But then he hasn't quite become used to the word queer meaning anything other than strange, or, in this instance, unwell. He's obviously aware of the use of the word queer to mean homosexual – but, like so many people of his generation, he hasn't quite caught up with the word gay yet.

It can happen to anyone.

In the recently published Andy Warhol's *Exposures*, Warhol tells an amusing story about an evening with Diana Vreeland, the doyen of the New York fashion world.

`One of the best times I had at Diana's was with the Duchess of Windsor. It was the first time I met the Duchess. I brought her a little flower painting. She thought it was a box of candy and kept trying to open it. I didn't know what to say or do, as usual.

`Diana's upstairs neighbour, Kitty Miller, the widow of the biggest Broadway producer in the thirties, forties and

39

fifties, was also there. The Duchess, Diana and Kitty were telling me how wonderful and glamorous life was in the good old days when their husbands were still alive. They said the flowers were gayer, the dresses were gayer, the parties were gayer. Everything was gayer but the men. It's funny how words change. For three solid hours the Duchess, Diana, and Kitty said "gay" every other adjective and never once meant homosexual.

`One time in Paris a rock star offered me a "blow" in the men's room at Maxim's. I thought he meant sex. But later I found out he meant cocaine. Later that night I saw Diana Vreeland at Regine's. She waved across the room and said, "Andy, give me a blow at five o'clock tomorrow." She meant the Telephone.'

In America, well-meaning friends warned me not to talk about "fags" when meaning cigarettes – to refer to someone as a faggot, is unfortunately, about the worst insult going and faggot, of course, handily abbreviates to fag. So to stand in a bar and say, "I'm desperate for a fag" could mean considerably more than a craving for nicotine.

Words from the gay vernacular – cottage, for example – cause moments of pause. Is the partner in conversation talking about some rustic retreat, beautifully thatched, with roses creeping around the door? Or is he talking about some public toilet in which he has experienced moments of bliss or, just as likely, moments of sheer horror?

The sixties didn't help language much, either – and the use of the word bread frequently makes me double think and wonder if the person who has no bread is meaning no bread, or is simply broke.

Of course the use of the word *he* in the preceding two paragraphs is considered in some political circles as the height of male chauvinism or straightforward sexism. Things have come to a sorry pass when the personal pronoun can cause offense – and when individuals no longer have gender, when chairmen and chairwomen become chairpersons or, horror of horrors, simply *chairs*. As Russel Baker put in a recent *New York Sunday Times* article: 'I recently met a chairperson. That is one of the advantages of living in the present age. Grandfather couldn't do that. I remember him sitting by the pot-bellied stove in the parlour one day in nineteen-ought-six moaning about the disadvantages of being born too soon.

`He had tramped all the way across the Short Hill Mountain that day and walked almost to Harper's Ferry. "Nary a chairperson, in the whole country," he said. "It looks like I'm going to die without ever seeing one." He did. He was born too soon.

Of course, it is just possible that this enrichment of language – some might consider it basic bastardization – may bring about a dramatic revolution in narrative writing. It is easy to envisage a future world in which all writing is totally without characters of any gender – instead of reading about Fred or Flossie, or he or she, we will read novels about persons who have become so divorced from identity that they (a safe word) will simple be noticed as *it*, or, if in the plural, as *they* or *them*.

Take down almost any volume from your bookshelves, gentle reader, and ponder some randomly selected passage for a moment or two. In your mind, transpose every vile sexist expression – neuter every *he* or *she*, render barren every *hers*, make impotent every *his*: think in terms of *theirs* and *its* – and see what enriched language is left.

As a writing person, I am amused – but appalled. Is this really what it is all about? Is it really even important? Let us hope not – and pray that the person trend can quickly be reversed before we all lose sense of sexuality and identity altogether.

GAY NEWS March 1980

ON BEING BASHED

At approximately 2am on the morning of Monday, March 15th I was queer-bashed as I walked home along Brighton sea front. Once I had managed to stagger home – by taxi, summoned by a reverse charge telephone call (I had no money on me), I went into what I can only describe as a kind of collapse. As I lay on my bed – bloody and shaken – the prime thought going through my mind was: What am I going to tell everyone?

I was blind drunk and fell over – perfectly possible, perfectly believable; I had tripped over the cat and fallen down stairs – not unlikely; I had been mugged – at least that *sounds* a bit better than being queer-bashed. A part of me did not want to admit what had *really* happened. But as the endless night wore on – and I didn't want to speak to anyone immediately, it was necessary to be alone and think at that point – I decided I had to admit the truth. It seemed important then, it still seems important now. Since the incident happened, I talked to a lot of people who – at some time in their past – have been attacked because they were gay. Very few have ever talked about it – and I suspect this is because of an awful sense of shame engendered because frequently assaults of this kind on gay men take place in or around areas notoriously used for cruising. As many gay men feel a sense of guilt about cruising, to be beaten up in circumstances which suggest the subject of the attack was cruising has about it the vague intimations of punishment meted out for behaviour that some people – at least – consider to be asking for it.

When I awoke from what a romantic novelist would call a fitful sleep, I could hardly move; both wrists were extremely painful and I was having difficulty lifting anything. A friend telephoned. I told him what had happened and described my various aches, pains and difficulties. "You sound as if you've got two broken wrists," he said. "I'm coming straight up. You'd better go to the hospital."

43

Some four hours later I tottered out of the Casualty at the Royal Sussex – one broken wrist in plaster, one sprained wrist in a support bandage. I had told the doctor that I'd tripped on a paving stone, fallen badly and, thus, caused the injuries myself. I didn't want to tell him what had really happened – just in case it had to be reported to the police. Like so many people I have no desire to be involved with the law. Had I admitted what had happened, however, I would probably have been given a full examination and not needed – as I subsequently did – to call out my doctor on two occasions (when I did tell him the truth.)

For most of the first day I was completely lucid, *too* lucid – telephoning the office to say I wouldn't be in, cancelling appointments and regaling friends with a lively and amusing after dinner story version of what had happened.

Then the shock hit me.

In the past, whenever I've read about shock, I've not quite believed it existed. Now I know that it does. For ten days, at least, it almost completely incapacitated me. I didn't really want to see people – though thoughtful friends trekked to the house of the friend with whom I was staying to see me. I didn't want to talk. I didn't want to eat – and subsisted for two weeks on a diet of jelly, fruit and yogurt. I stopped smoking – usually I get through between eighty and a hundred cigarettes a day. I stopped drinking – and now, four weeks later, I have still not touched alcohol. I couldn't write; I didn't want to read. Virtually all my bodily functions stopped – I didn't know if I wanted to pee and would simply guess that it was time to try. My reflexes had gone as a result of the shock, my doctor told me. Messages were not getting from my body to my brain. The boot in the kidneys couldn't have helped much, either, I'm not sure. I didn't want to go out – and am still pretty insistent that I have motorised transport or plenty of people with me when I go out at night.

"It is the nearest thing to the shock of rape a gay man can experience," one friend suggested. Though I'm not sure I fully endorse this statement, I know exactly what he meant. A victim of a queer-bashing assault has been subject to attack because of his or her sexuality in a similar – though very different – way as a woman subjected to rape. Someone else suggested that queer-bashing amounted to attempted murder – a view I consider a bit extreme. I can see the point though and suspect that it is sheer luck which prevents more gay men and women dying because of these attacks. I still think I was lucky; my attackers weren't armed. What happened to me could have been far worse.

What provokes the attack may seem obvious – a gay man (most usually) is found in a locale known for cruising (in Brighton that includes 'Sea Front promenade from West Pier to Black Rock swimming pool, night mainly', according to the *Spartacus Guide* – an enormous area along which any solitary male, gay or straight, can walk) and is beaten up by youths (usually) who are haunting the area for this purpose.

Of course, the reasons for their haunting an area known to be used by gays are difficult to fathom. Quite obviously a lot of people see gays as easy prey and treat us a form of blood sport; quite obviously a lot of people consider us as alien – and we all know what attitudes to aliens are. Some people who indulge in queer-bashing obviously believe they are reinforcing their butch image because they aren't too sure about it in the first place. Whatever reason may be suggested, it cannot be a complete answer. It is frightening that it happens – and confirms how much mindless hatred is still directed towards gays.

As I wrote (Hotspots, GN 237), being queer-bashed is something that happens to other people – or so I thought until, as they say in the movies, my number came up.

I had had a particularly good weekend. The house had swarmed with people. The Sunday had been particularly riotous – rather like an amateur production of Noel Coward's *Hay Fever* (with me as Judith Bliss). Food had been served, drinks had flowed, music had blared – it was the weekend of non-stop *Non-stop Erotic Cabaret*; letters had been dictated, articles written and discussed. Then we had drifted down to Bolts at Sherrys.

The amount of speed I'd consumed didn't help, of

course. Bolts at Sherrys closes at midnight. Friends had driven me home. No, they didn't want to come in for coffee or to talk. I went in alone and went to bed. But I couldn't sleep; I was rarin' to go. I got up again, dressed – and walked to the seafront. It was a windy and damply chilly night. There was no one around – but as I made my way up through the enforested Duke's Mound, up to the main road and home, I realised there *were* others about.

As I reached a confluence of pathways, I saw a figure and heard it say: "There's one of them." Instinctively, I knew I was in trouble. I doubled back the way I had come – thinking to make a hasty retreat along the beach road. As I reached the lower level, however, I saw that I was trapped.

I didn't know then – and certainly don't know now – how many people were involved in the attack. What struck me then – and what I remember now – is the sense that I was the prey. I felt that the youths – and I am sure they were very young – at the upper level were acting as beaters, flushing out anyone on any of the pathways and driving them down to the hunters who, it seemed to me, had every exit covered.

I think there were about ten youths in the area – and after an inelegant leap through some roadside bushes only two of them were near me. I am not at all an athletic person – nor ever have been; but slightly drunk and speeding, I hurtled off up the road. Blind panic and fear drove me on. Whilst I was moving, the blows were ineffective. On the floor, with, as they say, the boot going in, they were. Curiously, the verbal abuse was almost more painful. This was when it was made quite clear that I was being attacked because I was *queer*. I did fight back after a fashion, regained my feet and ran on a little further. Then I was down again. I continued to struggle and managed to get away again. Quite how I kept going, I don't know. Eventually I reached some steps and started to climb. Pursuit ceased – though I feared finding my assailants at the top of the stairs.

Once home I thought. I relived the experience again and again. I didn't realise that I was injured – though I knew I was bloody and bruised. I knew I could have telephoned friends and asked them to come up to the house; equally I knew I didn't want to see or speak to anyone. I wasn't ready for people. I couldn't believe what had happened had happened *to me*. Queer-bashing was something I'd read about – and now I realise, had rather casually dismissed. I can't say what being queer-bashed has done to me . . . but I still keep thinking about it *and wondering if it will happen again*. Maybe it won't to me . . . but the very nature of our society suggests it will continue to happen to others. And that's what's so frightening: the way we accept this kind of violence or knowledge of it against ourselves.

GAY NEWS April 1982

CHRISTMAS COMES

By the time the party comes around on December 24, the Christmas spirit is already beginning to wear thin. Office parties have brought out the sentimental ("I've always thought I might be a bit gay myself") or the savage ("Why *must* you queers go on about it?") in co-workers. Seasonal gatherings with close friends become strained as too much of a good thing causes natural bonds of decency and good manners to burst at the seams. For some of us, the worst is yet to come – semi-obligatory days locked in close confinement in the sagging bosom of the family.

And to compound the horrors of each individual's personal and professional involvements are the dominating *D*'s: *D*yspepsia – caused by over-indulgence in too-rich food; *D*runkenness – prompted by the un-natural bonhomie of the season; and *D*espair – provoked by the sense of physical ill-being from the first two *D*'s and by the sure knowledge that by January 2 an irate bank manager will be crossly complaining about the size of the overdraft that has been run up to pay for the festivities.

So – what to do?

Like Ebenezer Scrooge in Charles Dickens' *Christmas Carol*, we can try responding to cheery seasonal greetings with "Bah! Humbug!" – but it's a ploy that rarely works. Christmas – after all – is the one time of the year when we are honestly expected to feel good will towards all men and to have a good time if it bloody well kills us.

The burying-your-head-in-the-sand (basic *O*strich) position doesn't work either. Christmas won't go away – however much you pretend it isn't there.

Stop sending cards and see what happens: the gesture will pass unremarked for at least the first decade. Friends and foes alike will bury your doormat beneath a pile of missives which drive you to shriek a bitter "Ho, ho, ho" and reach for *another* bottle of your favourite tipple.

Try announcing that you will be ignoring Christmas Day completely, that you will dine simply on a boiled egg and a pot of Earl Grey. You won't be believed. Friends will laugh at your latest eccentricity; enemies will declare that you've always been a party-pooper.

And don't expect economics to be a means of rescue. Indicate you cannot afford to buy presents and friends will nod with sympathy and kindly understanding. Come Christmas morning, you will find yourself loaded down with gifts, drowning in a sea of discarded wrapping paper. Your friends will glow in the warmth of their own virtuousness; you will feel like an absolute shit. It's *Hell*.

So – what to do?

Try being sensible. It sometimes works. But remember, being sensible needs an iron will. Fight off the confidences at the office party, they will only cause embarrassment in the New Year. Ignore the insults, they will be regretted even more. Try not to overload with food. Eat sparingly, but enough. Turn down the second helping of turkey and the extra hunk of Christmas pud. "Are you ill?" people will ask. "Is there anything wrong? Can I get you anything else?"

"I'm being sensible," you will stoutly answer – and just as stoutly stick to your guns as the hoots of derisive laughter ring in your ears.

Otherwise . . . well, it's dyspepsia and bromo-seltzer for you.

And how to cope with the endless drinking and the endless hangover which looks set to stretch from December 23 to January 2 – or thereabouts?

Try staying within the limits that you are used to – though that option is even more difficult than turning away food. People get offended – think you are being stand-offish, spurning their hospitality.

Worse, there's always the party joker who thinks it's fun to perk up your orange juice with just enough vodka to give the drink a kick without you noticing. It happens! There's nothing more disconcerting than the moment when you realise that your vision's gone, your words are slurring and your coordination's shot to pieces.

Or there's the other friend who declares "You're getting

soft. You can't take it like you used to in the Good Old Days." Be brave, admit the years have taken their toll; don't relent and get yourself into training for the Alcoholic Olympics.

Otherwise . . . well, it's rampant drunkenness, curative hairs-of-the-dog (basic *Anaesthesia*) and a shot liver for you.

And the expense of it all? Try caution, don't run riot with the credit cards and the overdraft. Try restricting the size of your present list and limiting the amount you will be spending on each person.

Otherwise . . . well, it's mounting debt and bleak despair for you.

Ultimately, years of experience have taught me that to attempt to ignore – or even soft pedal – on Christmas is wasted effort. There is no escaping.

This year, my home will be turned into a fairy grotto. Over-eating will be the name of *my* game, drunkenness will be what sends me to sleep. The dustbins will overflow with the detritus of the season's goodwill.

Be like me. Eat, drink, be merry . . . and suffer!

Ho, ho, ho.

HIM December 1983

GROWING UP GAY,
GOING GREY

Sometimes I am convinced by the conspiracy theory. Just recently, I casually remarked to my lover – some years younger than myself – that I needed to purchase a new pair of shorts before we went on holiday. 'I don't think men of *your* age should wear shorts,' he snapped decisively. 'Isn't it time you acted your age?'

I'm afraid it had never occurred to me that at the age of 38 I am beyond wearing shorts. Ho-hum . . .

A few days later, a female friend – approaching her middle 30s – was complaining to me that she didn't know the names of any of the current chart groups. She seemed surprised that I not only knew the names, but also liked and possessed many of the records.

A little later in that same week, I was spending the evening in a 'mixed' disco, accompanied by several straight friends and one other gay man. 'God I feel old in here,' one of the straight friends remarked.

He's 23, his girlfriend is a little older. Admittedly, most of the people around us were in the 16-20 age bracket. But I didn't feel 'old' – and nor did the other gay member of the party. *We* were both perfectly relaxed and comfortable as we drifted about the club.

Yet these events – spaced a mere matter of days apart – did make me wonder. Am I fooling myself? Am I making a *fool* of myself? Am I pretending to be something I'm not? Am I turning into that most dreaded of creatures – the perpetual teenager?

As soon as these unwelcome thoughts had filtered into my consciousness, I started to rebel. What's so great about 'acting your age'? What's so wonderful about being a mature person? What's so special about being out of touch? Why – at a certain age – should we be expected to abandon discotheques, say, in favour of sedate dinner parties and discreet cocktail-swilling gatherings?

I suspect that practitioners of heterosexuality have far

more pressures exerted upon them by society at large and by their families and peers in particular which stress the need to conform than do their gay counterparts. Thus, I could just about comprehend my friend's comment that he felt old in the company of the late teen crowd at the 'mixed' disco. Most of *his* peers have settled into steady relationships, marriages, careers and mortgages. The pressures for him to become a 'responsible' member of society are greater than they would be for a gay man of the same age – because the gay man exists, in many respects, outside that society anyway.

Yet most aspects of gay life tend to mirror heterosexual society – gay men have lovers (not wives), careers and mortgages. They have the same financial problems and similar emotional ones to their straight counterparts.

Yet gay man are frequently accused of being trapped within a Peter Pan syndrome – an emotional manifestation of a physical desire not to grow up, or, perhaps, the expression 'grow old' should be substituted for 'grow up'.

However, the desire to remain youthful – if not young – is not restricted to gay men. Growing old holds terrors for all of us.

I come back to the question: What's so great about growing up?

All too often the ageing process is a process of fossilization. All too often growing up seems to be an excuse to become rigidly and unbendingly set within a certain pattern of existence which allows no deviations for growth of either new ideas or new pursuits.

`I don't know the names of any of the current chart groups.' The very sentence is almost a proud boast. But why? What is there to be proud of in ignorance? What is laudable about letting yourself get out of touch? Why be party to the strengthening of the 'generation gap' just because our society believes that we should socialise with our peers, respect our elders and scorn those younger than ourselves because they have yet to maintain the 'maturity' which only age can bring.

For as long as I can remember, I haven't 'conformed' – I

have a chronic inability to treat with respect those who demand but do not deserve it; I have an innate loathing for formal attire – and if pressed into a suit and tie feel so constrained that I become another person; I dislike the hours we are expected to keep (by the very nature of licensing hours and the availability of public transport) and my natural rhythm runs counter to that by which most people exist.

Because I can write and, more importantly, make a living from what I write, I have, for almost the entire of my working life, been able to set the pattern of my days in a fashion *I* find pleasing. This in itself enables me to indulge in a lifestyle which isn't constricted by most of the more boring everyday conventions. Thus, I am able to balance my working hours against my hours of leisure.

As I firmly believe in the importance to our very well-being of leisure, I throw myself as wholeheartedly into pastimes as I do into work.

Sadly, many people consider the pursuit of pleasure immature – and certainly many of those who engage in 'political' activities within what can laughably be called the 'gay movement' are so trapped the British concept of the Christian work ethic that they totally deny the pleasure principle.

Unless we are born rich, all of us have to work to survive. But is work an end in itself? Or is work a means to an end? I would plump for the latter. I consider work a means to an end – that end being the financial ability to allow me to enjoy the pursuit of pleasure.

I am determined not to grow old gracefully – because the word 'gracefully' suggests gentility and stuffiness. Of the many older people that I have known, those who have been the most fun to be with have been those who have had riotous lives – working hard, perhaps, but seeking pleasure where they will. Most of them haven't 'acted their age'; most of them have been surrounded by friends younger than themselves – friends who have learnt from them and from whom they in turn have learnt.

I shall pad about the streets of Mykonos in my new

shorts regardless; though naturally my hair is streaked with grey, it will continue to change colour as I see fit and as I desire. Most importantly, I shall refuse to grow up – because I believe *that* is an end to the learning process and one of the great joys of existence has to be the act of discovering something new.

I will continue my pagan pursuit of pleasure – and thank such gods as may be that I am gay, because I firmly believe that one of the things we should celebrate about our difference is our ability to stay young for far longer than our straight friends.

Like Peter Pan, I will continue to take flight – in search of pleasures new and pastures as yet unseen. And I will scorn conformity and the dreary thought of 'acting my age'!

HIM December 1983

TOO MUCH OF A GOOD THING?

Promiscuous: the very word is emotionally loaded; but just what does it mean? Though *The Shorter Oxford English Dictionary* does not put any specifically sexual connotations on it, the sense is clear enough – 'That is without discrimination or method; confusedly mingled, indiscriminate'. In a purely sexual sense, particularly in relation to gay men – how do we view promiscuity?

Is promiscuity anti-social, encouraging the spread of sexually transmitted diseases? Is promiscuity an act of desperation by men who want to prove they can still get it up and still get it on? Is promiscuity something which provides reassurance by convincing the individual that he is still viable in the sexual market-place? or is promiscuity an act of rebellion against the established patterns of heterosexual society?

Should promiscuity be condoned or condemned – or applauded?

Each individual has his own views about sex 'without discrimination or method', random couplings with any available partner. Those who are whole-heartedly for it – American author John Rechy, for example – seem slightly hysterical in their self-justification. Those who oppose it seem almost equally hysterical in their attitudes.

But just how to define promiscuity?

What is the standard by which sexual behaviour can be assessed? Do we accept that the couple – in either hetero or homosexual terms is the norm? If we do, then that must mean that any deviation from a coupled existence is a promiscuous act.

But can we accept the couple as the norm? Might we not consider that two individuals bonded together by emotional or legal ties are only conforming to a set of rules applied by religion (in a British context, Christian) and the social order. Does the fact that Christianity restricts partners to one at a time (in a heterosexual context) and is basically opposed to homosexual relationships mean that the Moslem (who can have more than one wife and in whom homosexual behaviour is at least tolerated) is promiscuous?

The very term 'promiscuous' slips and slides away from us the more we consider it and at a very basic level the word can only be defined to mean sex with any number of partners. Certainly not indiscriminate sex – as however casual the process of selection, even for one night stands most people make a conscious act of decision. And the act of definition really depends on each individual.

What one of us may consider promiscuous, another may think perfectly ordinary sexual behaviour.

Practically the only major published defence of promiscuity within a homosexual context appears in John Rechy's *The Sexual Outlaw* (1977). To my mind, this is a remarkably silly book which seeks (sexual) political justification for acts of motiveless physical gratification.

'The promiscuous homosexual is a sexual revolutionary,' writes Rechy. 'Each moment of his outlaw existence he confronts repressive laws, repressive "morality". Parks, alleys, subway tunnels, garages, streets – these are his battlefields.

'To the sexhunt he brings a sense of choreography, ritual and mystery – sexcruising with an electrified instinct that sends and receives messages of orgy at any moment, any place.'

Later in the same chapter, Rechy continues to romanticise the promiscuous gay man. 'In this context the sexual outlaw flourishes. The pressures produce him, create his defiance. Knowing that each second his freedom may be ripped away arbitrarily, he lives fully at the brink. Promiscuity is his righteous form of revolution.'

This all seems like typical American overstatement. Worse is to come. '"You have an untested insurrectionary power that can bring down the straight world,"' Rechy wants to tell an audience to whom he is lecturing. '"Use it – take the war openly into the streets. As long as they continue to kill us, fuck and suck on every corner! Question their hypocritical, murderous, uptight world."

`But I don't say that. Why?

`Because promiscuity, like the priesthood, requires total commitment and sacrifice.'

Of course, various things have to be borne in mind when considering Rechy's hyperbolic remarks. Firstly, John Rechy, through a series of autobiographical novels which commenced with *City of Night* (1964) has proved himself to be one of the most narcissistic authors America has ever produced. His books are about promiscuity as a form of self-flattery. Thus, this raises the pertinent question: Is promiscuity about ego? Patently so in Rechy's case. And a book like *The Sexual Outlaw* – as a defence of a random and casual approach to sex – becomes worthless when it is considered simply as a self-justifying ego-stroking.

In the Rechy context, promiscuity is a political act and this implies that the promiscuous gay male is consciously or subconsciously making a statement to the world at large every time he enters a cottage, park or some other cruising area in search of instant-sex.

British commonsense provokes me to pooh-pooh this ridiculous American notion.

Take away Rechy's schoolboy romantics and half-baked theorising and what is left: A promiscuous individual who wants to disguise the fact that he is still proving to himself that he's a viable commodity in the sexual market-place.

A sexual revolutionary? Certainly not!

Rechy's age is something of a dark secret; the internal evidence of his books suggests he must be approaching fifty. Does this suggest that promiscuity is a particular province of the older gay man?

Things would be much easier if classification of the promiscuous were that simple. Awkwardly, promiscuous acts mean different things within specific sets of circumstances and within specific social groups.

For example, if a youth new to the gay scene is promiscuous does that mean a) that he is simply indiscriminate or (more likely) b) that he is behaving like a kid let loose in a sweetshop and grabbing as many goodies as he can because this is the first opportunity he's had to experiment in this way?

In heterosexual circumstances, promiscuity cannot hope to compete with the volume of numbers which are considered promiscuous in gay circles. Neither heterosexual men, nor heterosexual or gay women indulge themselves to anywhere near the same degree as gay men. At a very basic level, none of these three groups has the amount of opportunity for sexual expression open to them as do gay men.

But at what number of sexual partners can a gay man be considered to have moved from the sexually active to the sexually promiscuous? Who can say? That kind of body-counting leads to all sorts of artificially applied rules and all kinds of unpleasant moralising.

And body counts don't even begin to consider the different levels of sexual drive possessed by any group of individuals. To one man, daily sexual encounters may be the norm. If those encounters are with the same person, he's highly sexed; if they're with a different partner on each occasion, he's promiscuous. Yet to another man, sexual encounters at widely spaced intervals may be all he requires. because levels of sex drive differ, should he who needs physical gratification on a more regular basis be accused of promiscuity?

And the word has an accusatory ring to it; by no stretch of the imagination can the word promiscuous be considered as a flattering adjective.

It's extremely possible and highly likely that when one individual accuses another of promiscuity, there is more than a hint of envy involved. Yet it is an obvious fact: promiscuous behaviour *is* condemned.

Heterosexual moralists use the promiscuity of the male homosexual as a whip with which to flog him; liberal trendies disguise their shock by adopting a pose of amused admiration; gay men speak with scorn of their promiscuous compatriots – though possibly carrying on in a similar manner in circumstances they hope won't be detected. All of which suggests the subject of promiscuity is surrounded by an obscuring wall of hypocrisy.

Maybe we all *secretly* long to be promiscuous; to get it on with every man we desire. Maybe it is only the constriction with which we have grown up that restrains some of us. Aren't gay men as conditioned as their straight counterparts into thinking in terms of all the conventions of romantic fiction: true love, marriage of a sort and a relationship which will last until 'death do us part'?

So if that premise is accepted, isn't it obvious that a lot of the fear and guilt and snide remarks about promiscuous behaviour stem from our essentially heterosexual conditioning? Yet when that line of reasoning is turned around, is there anything wrong about wanting the stability of an enduring relationship? Surely the only fault lies with those who are too quick to condemn in others what may be a legitimate form of expression and communication.

To be or not to be promiscuous? It is a personal choice which may be dictated by any number of sets of emotional, physical or intellectual circumstances.

At this stage of the game, I've realised one thing about promiscuity: writing about it impersonally is impossible. All I can set down is a series of questions – the answers to which I do not know. I find I cannot *exactly* define what it is I mean when I describe someone as promiscuous and I wonder why I use the term in the first place.

I know people I consider promiscuous, who spend almost all of their spare time hunting for sexual partners. I know I view these constant cruisers, with their ceaseless appetites for sex with incomprehending amazement. Some of these friends – I consider – are promiscuous out of a sense of desperation; others act promiscuously because it is a basic physical expression of their loneliness. All of those I know and think of as promiscuous are of a certain age and they have made the sacrifices Rechy speaks of: sex comes before everything else. Friends go by the board because they stand in the way or interfere with the pursuit of sex. To me, it's incomprehensible. But maybe that's because I long ago opted for a different way of life.

Up until the age of about twenty-eight, I would consider myself as promiscuous. The past ten years have been swallowed by work, by work related socialising, by work related activities. I *think* that such time to myself as I have is most happy when shared with friends. Developing and sustaining relationships with friends has somehow precluded much sexual activity. I like to think that that's the way I want it.

But am I fooling myself? I am as aware as the next man that short chubby men of nearly forty aren't most men's ideal of the sexually desirable. Did I stop being promiscuous because I was unsure of my sexual viability? In other words, did I opt out for the soft option, a course that so far as my ego is concerned is safer?

When I express incomprehension and amazement at the promiscuous behaviour of others – am I expressing some kind of subliminal envy? Am I being hypocritical? Do I mock something solely because I fear that I can no longer do it?

Are most of our responses to promiscuity dishonest? Because of religious taboos and social stigmas and personal guilt and fear?

I do not know. Like everything about sex, promiscuity is a great question mark; it is a set of thoughts, beliefs – what-have-you – which will never crystallise so long as there is a thought in my head. Approaches and attitudes change all the time. I am no longer the same person I was when I wrote the first line of this article; I have changed my views of promiscuity several times.

Is the promiscuous man getting too much of a good thing? Or is the man who is cautious in his sex life not getting enough of something wonderful?

I don't know . . .

Do you?

HIM February 1984

DRESSING UP

`In the past only the minority of homosexuals who wanted to resemble the members of the opposite sex were easily identifiable. Most straights therefore believed that all gay men wore markedly feminine styles and all gay women dressed in men's wear,' writes Alison Lurie in *The Language of Clothes*. 'Today, when they are out of the closet, it is apparent that most homosexuals dress like everyone else, at least when in mixed society. Many gay men, in fact, have now adopted the "macho look", and to the casual observer seem more masculine than most heterosexuals.'

The Western society into which most of us have been born still maintains a series of quaint superstitions about clothing – for example, female babies should be wrapped in garments in shades of pink; male babies should be bundled into clothes in shades of blue.

This same hand-me-down wisdom decrees that little girls wear frocks and skirts and little boys wear shorts and trousers. In some societies, however, exceptions can be made – the fact that a skirt (the kilt) is the traditional form of dress for the Scots male is not taken as any sign of effeminacy – though it would be considered as such south of the border.

With the approach of maturity, most young women adopt the use of cosmetics to either enhance or disguise aspects of their face – in a ritual which is as much about competitiveness with other women as it is about attraction of men. If a young man were to do the same he would find himself at least derided for rampant eccentricity, most likely condemned as a freak.

As the nature of our society slowly changes and as the position of women within that society has altered, trousers as an item of feminine attire have become widely accepted – though only when the women wearing trousers are within the context of relationships with men. Take the men away and the picture changes completely – for then women in trousers are condemned as lesbians aping men

63

and, as such, a threat to (heterosexual) men.

The idea of men wearing frocks or skirts is still totally unacceptable. Sure, it's okay within a show-business framework – and drag performers like Danny La Rue probably draw the bulk of their adoring audience from heterosexual society. Sure pop performers like Boy George and Marilyn may adopt a semi-drag dress-style – but again, they're safe because they're entertainers and, as such, fulfil a ritual role which has its roots in religious observance and can operate without the rules of society. It is part of their job to be larger than life, outrageous, different.

The average male donning a frock in the Boy George style and applying make-up with the precision of Marilyn would be viewed as an object of contempt – be he gay *or* straight – simply because aping women is considered a denial of masculinity, still a very highly valued commodity in society at large in virtually all areas of the world.

It would be gratifying to believe that once an individual has determined the nature of his or her (homo) sexuality, one of the first things they would leave behind them (part of the excess baggage of heterosexual assumptions) would be the attitude of society at large towards aspects of dress. Curiously, this doesn't seem to be generally true. In fact, in many instances, these beliefs and the taboos which support them appear to be even more rigidly enforced in homosexual society.

There are two ends to the vast spectrum of recognisable male gay dress styles (which, for the sake of simplicity, will be concentrated on here) – both representing extremes and each viewed with a certain level of contempt for the other.

The classic heterosexual stereotypical male is fey, feminine and limp wristed. Good for a laugh – like the character played by John Inman in *Are You Being Served?* or Melvyn Hayes in *It Ain't Half Hot Mum*. It is, however, interesting to propose that in gay terms the stereotypical gay male is rather different. For a considerable number of gay men, the supposedly macho supermale look – the denim or leather clone – has become something of a stereotype, something of a joke. The super-butch image – jeans, workshirt, boots, moustache – suggests homosexuality far more than does an essentially 'soft' dress style. And because some gay men have so much exaggerated maleness – with heavier boots, extravagantly worn jeans and even bigger and bushier moustaches – they are representing a kind of comic opera version of masculinity which can rarely survive the removal of the uniform.

Do clothes make the man? Does the act of dressing-up to conform with an established sexual image (Tom of Finland drawings come to life) mean that the physical and emotional responses follow suit? It seems unlikely. The truth is probably more painful – that the macho disguise is a simple sexual lure that has to be shed with the costume, leaving an average being who then has to work even harder in bed with his selected sexual partner so as to fit the image rather than disappoint. Few of us have the physical dimensions or the sexual staying power of those comic book bedroom athletes so much emulated or possess the *total* level of masculinity which implies endless satisfying penetration and protection. To conform completely to the image must be impossible – and if the latter is true, then a lot of gay men must find themselves contending with a self-imposed set of sexual problems.

Implicit in the clone mentality is a fear of softness – of a part of their nature which might be read as feminine. At the more extreme end of this type there is a conservatism and a rigidity which relies on as many keys and colour codes as a Masonic Lodge or a Boy Scout troupe. To be specifically categorised in a sexual sense implies a lack of imagination, any sense of the excitement of exploration and a denial of areas of self-discovery which are vitally important.

At the other end of the spectrum discussed above are those who have adopted a totally soft style. Yet this softness – and the camp which so often accompanies it – also makes a set of statements.

Those who adopt a soft (camp, if you like) style – clothes without the hard masculine edges – appear to do so (consciously or sub-consciously) in reaction against a dominant and repressive masculinity which pervades men, and women (Margaret Thatcher, for example) alike, the self-appointees of Authoritarianism. An interestingly large percentage of those who opt for the soft option can be characterised by age – they are usually a good generation away from those who have taken on the colouring of the super-butch.

But do this group of gay men adopt softer – more feminine approaches – as an initial act of rebellion against up-bringing and background or against the generation of gay men who have preceded them and who have themselves adopted a style of dress which suggests authority because of the heavy masculine tones implicit in the macho look?

Certainly those who wear what have come to be known as street-style clothes – culled from second hand shops, flea markets, jumble sales, attics and regenerated with the use of native wit and imagination – possess a uniform every bit as identifiable as that of the clone. In this instance, however, style and fashion play a part – and once a street style has been taken up by those who manufacture for the High Street shops, then the original wearers will create a new look which, in turn, will percolate upwards and outwards.

The implicitly sexual message encoded in the clothes worn by gay men at this end of the spectrum are far harder to read than those more obviously displayed by the clone and his sub-species. If these messages can be read at all, they do not directly state preference for specific sexual acts. Softness, camp and femininity cannot be read – within this group – as indications of bedroom passivity. Experience suggests that this group can be as malely aggressive as those wearing the more patently apparent trappings of super-butch.

Those who are unafraid of camp and what is generally spoken of as the feminine side of their nature seem to be far more assured about their sexuality; to feel less need to impose a disguise on their natural selves. But maybe this is because they have grown up into or are growing up into a world which at some levels at least seems less hostile to gay men than that in which the preceding generation grew up.

And, of course, when talking about the extreme ends of the spectrum – the super-butch clone and the feminized male – it is easy to forget the areas in-between. The middle of this arc of style certainly includes far more gay men than the outer limits – gay men who neither wish nor need to go to extremes, men who merge with the crowd and almost certainly consider their more visible compatriots outlandish and excessive.

Yet we are judged on extremes and we judge on extremes; the signals which reach our brains from the messages that are coded into the clothes we wear must most usually be inaccurate. Rather than concentrate on the outward style, we should look for the being beneath the fancy dress.

Seeing should not be believing and the dressing-up which has become so much of an outward show of the male gay scene should be taken as no more than a masquerade. Beneath the mask may be someone completely different.

HIM June 1984

MIDDLE-AGED SPREAD:
A RIPOSTE

God! Only a year off forty and another two teeth gone forever. If things continue at this rate, it'll be dentures and Sterodent for me before too long. Oh well, it's all part of getting older, drifting into middle-age. God! I'm putting on weight. I'll have to go on a diet. Cut out all those pints of Guinness and those endless gin-and-tonics. Oh well, I suppose middle-age goes with middle-aged spread.

But will those humpy numbers still fancy me? I doubt it. Or maybe I'm just not bursting with what I always think of as sexual confidence.

God! I feel tired. A pile of books to read for review depresses me. A stack of records to listen to for review bores me. And the pad full of notes for various articles for future issues daunts me. Shall I go out? Whisk myself down to one of the local gay pubs, bars or clubs? Maybe not. It's all a bit of a slog. Expensive, tiring – and probably boring to boot.

Anyway I must economise. There are the repayments to make on the bank loan, a crippling tax bill to be settled, the telephone, gas and electricity bills have just arrived. The rates and water rates need paying. I could do with some new clothes – but can't really afford them. I could do with a raise – but am too nervous to ask for one. The house needs repainting, re-wiring and something doing about the damp. It'll have to wait. The cat doesn't like being put on a diet – but money has to be saved somehow.

I feel ill. I keep throwing up. Do I have stomach cancer? I think I'm going deaf – or is it the fact that people just mumble? Are those pains in my chest a heart-attack? Or am I smoking too much? Are those blinding headaches a brain tumour – or just a hangover? My doctor tells me I'm A-OK. I'm *not* reassured. My optician tells me it's time I went in for another eye-test. It's years since I had my last pair of glasses. Does he know something I don't.

If I have sex – will I catch AIDS? If I don't have sex – will

I die of frustration? Why do I always fall in love with the wrong man? Why won't the right man fall in love with me?

Middle-age. Are there really another forty years of this?

Am I suffering from the booze, de blues – or a mid-life crisis?

It certainly can't be the latter – surely Roger Baker told us that gay men don't have mid-life crisis in his article of the same name in these columns only last month.

Well, I for one don't believe him.

In his article, Roger Baker baldly states, "This 'male menopause', or 'mid-life crisis' as they call it in the States was, if it happened at all, a result of lifestyle and *not* some medically defined phase that happens to all men. And that lifestyle is one in which gay men take no part. Even if we happen to be middle-aged, middle-class and in middle-management, because we're also gay we are inevitably free from certain pressures put on heterosexual men in the same position."

Too much emphasis is placed on the *style*; not enough awareness is shown of the *life*. Anyone can have a style – it's not some exclusively gay or straight preserve (though it will vary from individual as taste, inclination and income dictates). Equally – and more importantly – we all have a life that has to be led and led within a certain framework that is essentially the same whether we are hetero or homosexual.

In the broadest sense of the word, *all* human beings have to have homes (bed-sitters, flats, houses or palaces); all have to clothe themselves and all have to feed themselves. Most of us, in one way or another – contribute to essential service (gas, electricity, water rates, rates, telephone) bills. Most of us have to make some kind of contribution to the national budget – by way of our tax and other related payments, over which we have no control and precious little say.

Thus, in a very real (human as opposed to sexual) sense, gay men (and women) are under the same basic pressures of simple existence as heterosexual men and women. The only real difference – at a base level – that I can discern between gay and straight individuals is the nature of the sexual preference. And that's an end to the matter.

Sure, if we want to, we can accept a whole set of myths about gay life – for example, we can believe in the so-called 'Pink Pound' and the 'Pink Economy'. These fabled items are an invention of one or two ill-informed people who have media access and have happily propounded the fable that gay men have a high disposable income.

As it happens, I *do* know one or two rich gay men: I know quite a few gay men who can think of themselves as 'comfortable'; I know a lot of gay men who find budgeting a tight squeeze – and I know an awful lot of gay men who are downright poor. Except for the first category, I don't know anyone who has got money to throw around with *gay* abandon. Thus – it is my contention – that virtually *all* gay men are under the same major pressure as their hetero-sexual counterparts: financial worry. And worry is good for no-one.

Roger Baker's suggestion that because gay men are socially mobile they are less likely to feel envy of each other than straights seems totally spurious. As does his statement that, "the inevitable wide range of jobs and professions mixed within the gay world ensure that our professional lives rarely, if ever, impinge on our personal values."

Though social mobility is available to the gay man, most stay within a defined area (class background, educational, economic, style-sense). Equally, it seems foolish to presume that straights confine their personal lives and social acquaintances to those who move within exactly the same sphere. Equal opportunities is an expression much in favour at the moment – and certainly so far as social life is concerned, gay men and women and straight men and women have equal opportunities when it comes to the people they meet and the friends they make.

It is the central core of Baker's argument that is the most contentious. "Then there is sex," he announces. "Our mid-life crisis victim is apparently convinced that his sex-life is at an end. The capacity remains, the desire certainly does, but where are the partners with whom he can share again his urgency, excitement, vigour and romantic ideals? Hence the painful last fling with secretary or assistant."

71

Well, that seems to successfully dismiss the middle-aged heterosexual male . . .

But according to Mr Baker, things are very different for the homosexual male of middle years. "A gay man has no such problem where success is concerned," he emphatically declares. "For most of us, a vivacious and varied sex life has always been something we take for granted. And there is no reason why it should all suddenly stop at 40."

Phew! That's pretty hard to swallow – as the proverbial choirboy said to the bishop . . .

For starters – nothing should ever be taken for granted, least of all the possibilities of an endlessly "vivacious and varied sex life." And doesn't it all seem a bit self-deluding? Doesn't that simple declarative paragraph suggest someone ignorant of the realities of the lives of the vast majority of gay men?

The letters which appear on our own Vale of Tears page more than suggest that there are a large number of gay men who do feel that their sex lives *have* ended at the age of 40 – more depressingly, there are as many letters from far younger men who feel that their sex lives haven't even started.

It's all very well for sophisticated London journalists – writing for publications like *Forum* (Roger Baker is Editor) and *HIM* – to forget about the average gay man who hasn't spent years thinking about the politics and practicalities of gay sex. It is all very well for those of us in the trade (forgive the pun) to have our little theories and beliefs – but in the final analysis most of them bear little relation to real life.

Most gay men drag through their life the impedimenta of their social conditioning – most especially those gay men of Roger Baker's age 50) or, for that matter, of my own age (39). We grew up in a pre-Gay Liberation world – and at best can have only assimilated the theories and practices which have come along since our basic characters were formed.

Gay men – like straight men – have expectations and hopes and many of them are destined to remain unfulfilled. Our up-bringings condition us to look for love and enduring partners; exterior influences place a high value on sex and conquest. Because such a premium is put on youth – in both the straight and gay worlds – it is hardly surprising that so many men (of either sexual persuasion) feel defeated by the time they reach middle age.

But defeat and despair over matters sexual are not confined to those of us of advancing years. If all gay men were able to gain sexual gratification with the ease suggested by Roger Baker then our world would be a far different (possibly far happier) place.

But it doesn't work like that – and the Getting it on is Easy theory forgets all those who are shy or nervous in the established meeting places and all those who are more at ease with the anonymous (less traumatic?) contacts provided by cruising areas throughout the country.

Perhaps my main gripe with Roger Baker's article is the heavy emphasis on the importance to gay men of sex. *His* gay men are decidedly cock-eyed – and though I agree that a bit of jolly good rogering can't be beaten, I think there's more to life than that.

I also feel that 'The Mid-Life Crisis?' missed out totally on one area where heterosexual men of middle years have something of a cause to envy gay men in the same position.

Heterosexual relationships are rooted in marriage and often a mutual dependence which somehow excludes other people to a large degree. When one partner shuffles off the mortal coil, the other is too often left alone and isolated – with little or no contact with other people and with only limited interests.

The sometimes presumed impermanence of male gay relationships – far from leading to a lonely and despairing middle and old age – might well encourage more social inter-action with other people. This in itself means that some gay men – at least – can look forward to an old age which might not be vivaciously sexy but will be enriched by friendships nurtured and nursed over the years. To my mind, friendship is far more important than Baker's apparently vibrant sex-life.

I don't anticipate a particularly active or varied sex life

in the years to come. It's not that important, anyway. Maybe I'll feel randy, maybe I'll get frustrated. I can always have a wank. But I'll have my book, I'll have my records, I'll a slim-line cat and a stash of gin – and I'll have my friend. Oh – and I also expect I'll still have a bank loan, tax problems, rotting wiring, rising damp, peeling paint and all the other problems that are common to what is known as Civilised Man.

HIM July 1984

JEALOUSY

I'm jealous. I make no bones about that fact – though it isn't one of which I'm proud. I can look back down the years and even today shudder with embarrassment at some of the things jealousy has provoked me to do and say. There are friends and former lovers who can make my toes curl with horror when they make amusing stories of my jealous exploits – to which they were witness or of which they were victims.

Yet I can honestly say that I've never wanted to feel jealous and that after each attack of the emotion, I don't want to ever feel it again. But then, in a given set of circumstances – quite unbidden – there I am, seething with jealousy. Oh, how well I know the symptoms. How much I hate them.

When I'm jealous, I feel physically ill. In the past I have thrown up because of jealousy; on more than one occasion, the emotional pressure of jealousy has caused me to pass out. When in the clutches of this dreadful emotion, I am incapable of rational thought and – therefore – all but incapable of work.

Jealousy makes me the most dreary, depressing and frankly the most boring company. When I'm writhing in the grips of a passion, friends tend to shy away. They can't handle – and who can blame them? – the maudlin self-pity that often overtakes me. Drink doesn't help – though I incline towards the gin bottle as some kind of salve for my wounded ego.

And that's just the trouble. All too often, jealousy is an 'I' emotion. This unpleasant feeling usually centres around oneself. *I'm* hurt, I think to myself. *I'm* upset. How could he do this to *me*? Why is he treating *me* like this?

There can be few of us who haven't felt the pangs of jealousy. I should imagine it's one of the few really universal emotions. Most frequently provoked by a loved one, jealousy can be – often is – highly destructive. For the jealous lover is the one who most wants to hold his

75

beloved prisoner. By the very nature of things, prisoners want to escape. Within the context of a loving relationship, escape can mean only one thing: abandonment of the warder – the jealous over.

I most usually feel jealous within a sexual context. Why is my lover sleeping with someone else? Why is my lover sleeping around? In these circumstances there are a second set of questions which always follow the first. Is he bored with me? Can't I satisfy him? Doesn't he find me attractive any more? The second set of questions are about self-confidence and confidence with the relationship.

Now jealousy is a common human trait. But in gay terms it is also something more. When two men fall in love (or simply lust) they tend to continue to work within some kind of heterosexual relationship framework. As with most things, we – as gay men – are the products of the conditioning of the society in which we grew up. Because heterosexual couples are expected to be monogamous, we tend to accept the brief that we as homosexual couples should also have but one partner at a time.

Without going on at any tedious length about mens' sexuality, I'll simply say that men seem more naturally promiscuous than women and that, thus, two men settling down together have problems on their hands from the word go. If we didn't think in heterosexual terms – if we didn't equate love *and* sex within a relationship with success and love *but* infidelity within the same terms with failure – then we might be able to eradicate jealousy in gay partnerships.

But I should also make clear that sex isn't the only cause of jealousy – or at least in my own case. Sure, most usually it's a straying partner who gets me in an emotional tizzy. Yet sometimes jealousy is actually provoked by something at once far simpler yet far more complex. Bad manners.

It's a different sort of jealousy – and it's still based in the 'I' principle. However, in these instances – when I know the beloved is off with someone else and has completely forgotten to say he'll be home for dinner, I'm jealous and annoyed because the other person(s) have provoked him into acting thoughtlessly. I actually find being forgotten makes me far more jealous than being – to use a wonderfully old-fashioned term – 'two-timed'.

There has been one consolation over the years. When I was younger, jealousy took a distinctly physical form. I would shout and scream and throw things. On one spectacular occasion, I actually jumped out of a window. Now I've matured enough to keep my jealousy more-or-less under control. Inside, may be ready to implode – but generally, unless I'm goaded, I try to suppress any signs of the emotion.

Of course, it's not always possible. But I don't want to be known as a jealous guy – so I shall continue in my attempts to control this most messy of feelings.

HIM October 1984

THE COTTAGING TABOO

Cottaging, the pursuit of sex in public toilets, is the aspect of homosexual behaviour which most attracts attention from the law and which is subject to condemnation from both straight society and from large numbers of gay men and women who find the habit either distasteful or incomprehensible.

In the minds of those who think about cottages (though do not use them for sexual purposes), the image of the men who do use them as a means of making contact is fairly uniform: desperate and lonely men who are either too old or too unattractive to find partners in any other way. This is a misapprehension of almost cosmic proportions, as Laud Humphreys discovered when he was researching *Tearoom Trade*, an American study, first published in 1970, which remains the sole examination of this particular area of gay male sexual expression.

Unlike other aspects of gay life, the subject of cottaging has not attracted practitioners of the literary arts – though there is a memorable (and disquieting) scene centred around an arrest in the toilets in Leicester Square in Angus Wilson's *Hemlock and After* and a highly comic scene set in a public toilet in Roger Peyrefitte's *The Exile of Capri*. Cottages (tearooms in American) figure in Larry Kramer's *Faggots* and Andrew Holleran's *Dancer from the Dance*. Off stage cottages figure in the action of Michael Wilcox's *Rents*; on stage they were the location of Nigel William's *WCPC*, a hard-hitting attack on the police use of *agents provocateur*. Much of the dramatic tension of John Peacock's recently screened television play *More Lives Than One* centred around police entrapment and raids a on public convenience.

Yet as a phenomenon little consideration has been given to cottaging in either the straight or the gay press. Most of us read about cottaging only in connection with arrests; many of us show an often hypocritical lack of concern or consideration for those who have been arrested in a public toilet. Like male victims of queer-bashing, cottagers are often easily dismissed as 'asking for it'.

Those who cottage tend to do so covertly; there are few cottagers who are willing to come out of the closet about their habits and even the most inveterate wish to retain the anonymity which seems to be part of the attraction of this pursuit. For example, the cottager spoken to in connection with this article, though well-known on the gay scene, requested that his contribution go uncredited. Cottaging is not something practitioners want friends, family or employers to know about.

"There is a touch of the Zen 'happy accident' about cruising cottages," my informant told me. "One time you'll get home tired and frustrated after spending the day in freezing toilets and the next be on your way to an appointment with only minutes to spare and spend ten minutes of pure ecstasy just passing through. But of course, as I have recently learnt, there is increasingly the risk that it will turn out to be an unhappy accident."

There is a ritual quality about cottaging; there is also a whole mythology. Most of us must have heard stories about acquaintances – or *from* acquaintances – which centre upon an individual who sets out for a day of cottaging fully equipped with a note pad and pencil, a thermos of coffee and a pack of sandwiches. Many of us must have heard of legendary figures whose two week summer vacation was spent touring the cottages of – for example – the Lake District.

And therein must lie part of the attraction of cottaging: it can take place anywhere. The practised cottager has no need of a gay guide, he is not looking for bright lights and fast music. He's simply looking for men with whom to share a few fleeting moments of heightened sexual pleasure. All he needs is a toilet – and though it sometimes seems that public conveniences are edging slowly towards extinction, those who utilize them for sexual purposes know where to find them and most usually seem to know exactly which is currently popular, which is generally deserted and which is under police observation. There are those who can spot a plain clothes policeman or unmarked police car with as much facility as any stamp collector could a Penny Black in a box of all-sorts.

The ritual aspect of cottaging is interesting and for all but the most casual of cottagers seems an essential part of the game (and it should be noted that there are those who can tell cottaging stories with the kind of exactitude more usually associated with chess grand masters discussing moves in any given historical game). For those who operate from the lock-ups, a sheet of paper and something with which to write upon it are an absolute must. About the notes that pass from one cubicle to another there must – surely? – be an element of romanticism.

`I'm 25 and a brickie' scribbled on a page ripped from a pocket diary sounds decidedly more exciting than the perhaps more honest 'I'm 30 and a wages clerk with the council'. Because of the casualness and anonymity of the contact, fantasy can more easily be fulfilled.

And that brings us neatly to another of the fascinations of cottaging. Many a gay cottager has extolled to me the pleasures to be derived from a quickie in a toilet with a straight pick-up. Of course, much of this stems from succumbing to a fantasy. If one man is willing to indulge with another in – say – mutual masturbation, it seems more than likely that both of them have certain inclinations towards homosexuality. It just may be that circumstances prevent or forbid either one or both of them from fully exploring the potential of their sexual nature.

For it should be made perfectly clear, cottaging is far from restricted to 'desperate and lonely men who are either too old or too unattractive to find partners in any other way.'

In his foreword to the British edition of *Tearoom Trade*, criminologist DJ West (author of *Homosexuality*) comments: 'One might have expected that men indulging in anonymous sexual exchanges in lavatories would prove to be lonely, socially alienated, unmarried and possibly ageing homosexuals. In fact, it appears that the majority were married and predominantly heterosexual. They were seeking an additional sexual outlet that was quick, un-demanding and free from social entanglements. Fully committed homosexuals were less in evidence, perhaps because they had better means of making contacts and achieving satisfaction.'

While endorsing the first part of West's statement, it is difficult to agree with his concluding remark. And though one of the major tragedies of cottaging is the number of ostensibly straight men who find themselves arrested and confronting the horror and embarrassment of explaining their actions to wives (primarily) and employers; an equal part of the tragedy must be the same or similar situations which face gay men in the same position.

It is possible that men of whatever predominant sexual persuasion have been cottaging for as long as men have had the need to relieve themselves. "I sometimes wonder if the cottaging tradition goes back to primeval times," theorised my informant, 'when the boys might have hung around the downstream section of the watering-hole in the hope of sussing out a horny male who'd be happy to accept rapid relief."

We certainly have evidence (cited in H Montgomery Hyde's *The Other Love: An Historical and Contemporary Survey of Homosexuality in Britain*) that cottaging has flourished since the eighteenth century and that men caught in the act have been dragged before the courts since that time.

"Possibly it is merely the presence of water," continued my anonymous cottager, "hence the passion of gay men through the centuries for baths – from Rome, Athens and Kyoto through to New York and Amsterdam. It has even struck me that some spots in the world are so redolent of sexuality that even deserted or after some awful council modernisation there still remains a certain feel to them."

Possibly the simplest explanation of the attraction of cottaging is also the most obvious. Men using a public toilet for purposes of urination are also exposing the very organs which provide sexual pleasure and relief. Might it not be that they feel that whilst the penis is out it might as well be put to sexual use? Men seem to retain that schoolboyish interest in the dimension and appearances of the organs of others (if you show me yours, I'll show you mine) and even the most puritan must occasionally be overcome when in a public toilet by the temptation to peep. And after that? (If you let me feel yours, I'll let you feel mine).

Of course, these days peeping and feeling can be mighty risky pastimes.

"I suppose I was lucky. It wasn't until my early thirties that I suddenly experienced a series of traumatic, not to mention expensive and inconvenient unhappy accidents with the law. Until then I had thought how apt the word 'convenience'," my cottager explained. "I remember emerging from a very popular railway station toilet and the chap with me remarking 'if these people could see what they've just walked past, they'd turn blue!'."

The sense of danger and the risk of detection appears to add to the fun of the pursuit. "It all adds to the excitement – and the spontaneity – the weird detached quality," my informant pointed out. "Of course, for a long time it was difficult to see the funny side of it; we were dealing with a very serious business in those post-adolescent days. Man . . . was I keen! Later on, as I gained confidence as a person, I started to be able to be amused by it. *Sometimes*. The sight of an aspiring young professional in pin-stripes at 8.30 am on his way to a heavy day at the office buttoning his fly and desperately trying to remove the stains then dashing back into the rush hour crowd after giving head to three men through a hole in the wall can be very funny when you have a certain detachment.

"Attitude is important to some. The sneering going on sometimes puts you in mind of a competition for modelling gargoyles. But sometimes between two people there passes a kind of mischievous grin that makes up for the drabness."

Condemnation of cottaging is widespread. Straight society reads about a spate of arrests in public toilets in either their local paper or their Sunday tabloid and cluck in horrified disapproval. They immediately suspect that the men involved were preying on little boys (though what exactly constitutes a 'little boy' in their minds is open to doubt) and their memories of public conveniences convinces them of the shameless squalor of the whole thing. Gay men who condemn cottaging do so for a variety of reasons – the most readily used being that cottagers give the rest of us a bad name. Though on this count more than a shade of hypocrisy is probably operating because to my mind most gay men have had at least one convenient convenience experience.

Yet neither group pause to consider that amongst the cottagers may be fathers, husbands, sons and lovers – men who may be predominantly heterosexual, essentially bisexual, totally homosexual, completely unsure or simply frustrated. These men may be old and worn and lonely, they may be young and attractive yet trapped within an unsatisfactory marriage in which their partner cannot fulfil their sexual needs or fantasies, they may be little boys of sixteen or so who want contact with other men but don't know where to find them except in the stink of filthy toilets, they may be men who don't want the socially acceptable trappings of hearts and flowers romance.

Just possibly they have two things in common. Firstly they are *all* at risk from policemen – pretty or otherwise – who can haul them before the courts on the slightest pretext after spending hours, days watching the goings-on in a toilet. There's a waste of public money and a few bob Nigel Lawson could save if he had the inclination. Secondly, many of these men will be victims of prevailing sexual attitudes. It is currently fashionable to decry the so-called sexual permissiveness which flowered in the romantic days of the Swingin' Sixties. Yet that particular permissiveness was only for a few people – the well-heeled, the young, the beautiful. Most people don't know enough about sex to even consider being permissive and in some instances at least fear and ignorance drive men to cottaging because they dare not approach men in any other way.

Cottaging is one of the most contentious issues in gay society. It is easy enough to condemn; it is easy enough to condone if only by turning a blind eye and pretending it doesn't exist. Yet cottaging has always existed and will probably continue to exist so long as there is so much as a solitary male needing to relieve himself in a public place. it is an issue which should be confronted – rather than flushed out of sight in the toilet bowl of life.

HIM February 1985

DAVID BOWIE
THE MAN WHO INVENTED HIMSELF

Is David Bowie living in the shadow of a family curse? Has the schizophrenia of his step-brother been a major influence on the singer's work? Is he one of rock's major innovators? Or is he a clever manipulator who begs, borrows or steals the ideas of others? Is he homosexual, bisexual or heterosexual? Does any of it matter?

All of us are inquisitive; most of us have questions about our heroes which we'd like answered. We are interested in what it is that makes them tick; we are intrigued by the intimate details of their lives, most especially of their sex-lives. This is the very stuff that sells newspapers and books.

Yet the best we can hope for about many of the stars we admire is a series of interim reports; conjectural articles, unauthorised biographies. Occasionally a star will grant permission to a writer wishing to produce an accurate picture of a life which has the full imprimatur of the subject. Yet this is a path strewn with pit-falls – not least because *they* have the final say about what may or may not appear in print.

In the world of rock 'n' roll the most written about performers are Elvis Presley, the Beatles and The Rolling Stones. Coming up fast, in fourth place, is David Bowie – subject of a string of books which appeared last month. Already a biography scheduled for publication next year has been serialised in a leading newspaper, yet another unauthorised study is already underway.

Rogers and Cowan – Bowie's publicists – are less than thrilled. "There's only one person who can tell the story," a spokesman for the company snapped at me, "and that's David Bowie himself." Yet with his self-protective mania for privacy, it is unlikely that Bowie will pen an auto-biography. And with his well-known passion for altering the facts of his life, it is unlikely that Bowie would ever produce a totally honest book about himself.

In the end, the interested must interpret the available facts for themselves. Of the baker's dozen books that are around, only two have been written by people who were close to the singer – Angela Bowie's *Free Spirit* and Kenneth Pitt's *David Bowie: The Pitt Report*. This latter title offers any future biographer a wealth of fascinating data about Bowie up until he parted company with manager Pitt at the time of the success of 'Space Oddity'(1969).

Ultimately, however, anyone interested in David Bowie will create their own image, utilising the facts so that they accord with their own personal impression.

David Bowie was born David Robert Jones in Brixton, London, on January 8th 1947. This fact is unalterable although Bowie, early in his career, suddenly added a year to his age by giving his birthdate as January 1st 1946. It was a typical piece of fiction which has been followed on many occasions by similar efforts to distort facts and create a bizarre mythology.

As David Jones, he began his career at the age of 15 with a group known as the Kon-rads. He was still, at that stage, a pupil at his local Technical High School in Bromley – a London suburb to which Bowie's family had moved in 1953.

The Kon-rads, like most groups at the time, played cover versions of Top 10 hits by established stars like Cliff Richard and Chuck Berry. And just like The Beatles a year earlier, the Kon-rads were rejected by Decca after playing an audition in 1963.

Over the next three years, David Jones joined three groups in turn – the King Bees, the Manish Boys and the Lower Third, playing a combination of soul, R & B and rock. It was whilst singing with the Lower Third that Jones changed his name to Bowie – after the Texas adventurer Jim Bowie, who popularised a hunting knife. "I thought it was a ridiculous name," says lead guitarist Denis Taylor in a new book on Bowie. "I said it would never catch on."

Members of the group were also unimpressed with Bowie's insistence on 'mod' styles and make-up. "He seemed to become more effeminate," says the groups drummer Phil Lancaster. "That frightened the life out of me. To me, that was being queer."

But Bowie persisted and by 1966 he formed his own band called the Buzz. This band, we are told, was basically a backing group for the emerging talents of David Bowie himself.

It was from that point, certainly, that David Bowie began to create the unique characteristics which later made him a sensational but ambiguous star. In 1969 he made his personal breakthrough with a stunning solo song called 'Space Oddity' – released on the eve of the US moon landing in July 1969.

From the time of that breakthrough, Bowie has never looked back. He has become, not just a successful recording artist, but a powerful and curious *phenomenon* who has dominated styles for a long period and who later expanded his huge reputation by becoming an accomplished actor.

But who is this mysterious creature who created so many images? Can we distinguish between the man and the myths he has formed? Is it possible to understand his lyrics or to paint an accurate picture portrait of a Brixton boy who now lives as a rich recluse in Switzerland?

David Bowie's own comments about his background and influences provide few clues and many misleading remarks. His biographers have obviously been baffled by a long trail of falsehoods.

Because the roots of Rock & Roll are in black music, white rockers tend to emphasise their working-class origins. Bowie's published pronouncements have tended, quite falsely, to heighten the roughness of Brixton – indicating that those living in the neighbourhood were living on the frontline long before the area had become strife-torn. But most British rock singers allow themselves the luxury of this bit of mythologising, wishing to kick over any traces that may betray a less than lower-class background.

Bowie has sometimes claimed that he and his stepbrother Terry Burns spent the two years between 1955-57 living on a Yorkshire farm with a paternal uncle. But Terry, a clear decade older than Bowie, is on record as saying that this is a fiction, pointing out that he (Terry) was doing his

National Service at the time.

At least one study, *Alias David Bowie*, by Peter and Leni Gillman, has concentrated very heavily on the influences over Bowie of his step-brother. They stress that Terry's schizophrenia – which led ultimately to his suicide earlier this year – has been a frightening looming shadow from which Bowie has been fleeing all his life. These authors have unearthed a history of mental instability in Bowie's mother's family and seem to link Bowie's essential avoidance of Burns with his own fear that he too might be in danger of going insane.

Much has been made of the album title *Aladdin Sane* (A lad insane); considerably less attention has been paid to the fact that Bowie originally intended to call the album *Love Aladdin Vein* (love a lad in vain) which has a completely different set of resonances (possibly homosexual; suggestive of emotional coldness).

Of course, the question that has long been of abiding interest to journalists, biographers and fans alike is that of Bowie's sexuality. Is he or isn't he gay? As early as 1969, his manager Ken Pitt had decided to cultivate a gay following for Bowie. Jerry Hopkins has suggested that Pitt then telephoned the editors of the British gay press in an attempt to get them to promote Bowie to their readers. This is errant nonsense – because at that time there was but one gay publication that Pitt would have approached, *Jeremy*, then selling itself as a bisexual magazine for the bisexual sixties. An interview appeared in the January 1970 issue, but about the most outrageous remark made by the singer was that "I don't feel the need for conventional relationships." Within the context of the magazine, it was quite daring. But, equally, it could be taken to mean almost anything.

Bowie's famous statement about homosexuality came two years later. During the course of an interview with Michael Watts of *Melody Maker*, he declared "I'm gay and I always have been, even when I was David Jones." But was this as calculating a publicity ploy as the frocks he'd been wearing since the release of *The Man Who Sold The World* six months earlier? Who knows? Certainly by the time of the announcement, Bowie had been married to Angela Barnett for almost three years and his son Zowie (who now prefers to be known as Joey) was eight months old.

Though he'd had a hit with 'Space Oddity', at this time Bowie had a limited following. He wasn't exactly a star – and the furore over the Watts interview coincided neatly with the availability of *Hunky Dory*, released the previous month. A lot of claims have been for Bowie as a gay performer and as a gay lyricist. Serious examination of the complete canon of his work is revealing. Aside from songs like 'The Width of the Circle' on *The Man Who Sold The World*, 'Queen Bitch' and 'Andy Warhol' on *Hunky Dory* and 'John I'm Only Dancing' (1972 single), there's not much that can be accurately described as a 'gay song'. There certainly aren't statement songs like the gay Tom Robinson's anthem 'Glad to be Gay' or the heterosexual Rod Stewart's implicit statement song 'The Killing of Georgie'.

It's all too easy to take *too* seriously the remark made to interviewer Cameron Crowe during a 1976 session which became part of a subsequent *Playboy* interview. "When I was fourteen, sex suddenly became all important to me. It didn't really matter who or what it was with, as long as it was a sexual experience. So it was some pretty boy in class in some school or other that I took home and neatly fucked on my bed upstairs."

Didn't we all? And at that age isn't same sex easier to obtain than gratification with someone of the opposite gender?

Accepting the premise that Bowie is/was bisexual is fine; it's also interesting to consider that he may well have used the homosexual side of his nature as an aid to getting what he wanted. The relationship with mime artist Lindsay Kemp obviously fulfilled an intellectual need. The relationship with Mercury Records executive Calvin Mark Lee may have helped Bowie get the recording contract for 'Space Oddity'.

Bowie is one of those individuals who seem to find the person he needs at just the right moment. He is like a magnificent carnivore, gnawing his way through and gaining sustenance from the intellects or interests of others.

Thus Terry Burns introduced him to Kerouac's *On The Road*; from Kenneth Pitt's Oscar Wilde first editions and rare book collection he moved to the novels of Genet by way of the influence of Lindsay Kemp and the musical use of William Burroughs' cut-up technique via a meeting with the American author. Most of Bowie's influences are pretty obvious – the kind of icons who are discovered and rediscovered by generation after generation of vaguely intellectually pretentious suburban kids. Where Bowie differs from so many of his peers and his imitators is that he is capable of absorbing, sponge-like, a wealth of influences and regurgitating them in a way that is individual and likely to capture and recapture public imagination.

A highly skilled media manipulator, David Bowie learnt during a long apprenticeship the value of a striking image and a startling quote ("Hitler was a terrible military strategist. But his overall objective was very good. He was a tremendous morale booster." , "I don't think I've done anything decadent in the last six months." , "Freud would have a heyday with me." and – most tellingly – "Sometimes I don't feel as if I'm a person at all. I'm just a collection of other people's ideas."). Bowie, noted for possessing a low interest span, has long been aware of one of the cardinal rules of pop – that the record buyers are fickle, that the flavour of the month is just that, changes are all important. Throughout his career Bowie has known when to make the change, when to be one step ahead of fashion. With his two most recent albums, *Let's Dance* and *Tonight*, he made the biggest change of all – for with these and the *Serious Moonlight* world tour, Bowie made the transition from fashionable trendsetter to middle-of-the-road performer.

He'll be around for a long time yet. And the endless analysis will continue. But is it important? Not really – because in the end what matters is the music.

GAY TIMES June 1985

GREAT EXPECTATIONS

All relationships start with expectations. For the hetero-sexual couple, a burgeoning relationship will carry with it the implicit promise of marriage and living together – happy-ever-after – until the death of one or other of the partners. However the very institution of marriage is encumbered with a set of pressures – essentially to do with finance and success – which must impair the chances of the union succeeding from the outset. My hypothetical heterosexual couple do start their life together with the approbation of both family and the society in which they live. From the outset, they will have been encouraged to become and remain a couple.

By the very nature of their relationship, a same sex couple will have been discouraged to establish themselves as a kind of family unit. Families may well be actively hostile; society will certainly refuse to acknowledge the relationship and the many incentives which exist to propel heterosexuals into marriage – housing, tax relief, for example – are not really available for gay men or gay women living together as mates. The pressures on a gay relationship can be intense – because while the gay man or woman will have the same financial needs and the same desire for success as their heterosexual counterpart, they also have to contend with the general disparagement of the system in which they live.

Yet it is my contention that successful homosexual relationships can often prove far more stable and reward-ing than those of heterosexuals.

To my mind, heterosexual marriages can be viewed as a one way street down which unwitting couples blindly drive only to discover that they are in a cul-de-sac with no means of easy exit. Effectively, many married couples isolate themselves within the imprisoning confines of marriage and the family – becoming so absorbed in themselves and any off-spring they might produce that to all extents and purposes they cut themselves off from any

93

useful contact with the rest of the world. Because of the twoness of marriage and the endless demands of children, the heterosexual couple may find themselves – willingly or unwillingly, happily or unhappily – in a situation that allows few outlets for *self*-expression or *self*-discovery. Everything exists in tandem. If this situation prevails, separation, divorce or more dramatically death can be traumatic. Expertise at social intercourse can easily be lost if it is not practised with regularity.

It is my (cynical) view that gay couples (particularly *male*) have slightly less expectations of a relationship from the very outset. Once the gay man or woman has reached that plateau in life from which they can safely acknowledge their own sexuality, their own difference from the teeming mass around them, then he or she can start making conscious decisions about the pattern their life will take. They will quickly know that they will not marry, they will readily admit that they are unlikely to have children – though both male and female will be capable of the acts and processes which engender children. Thus two of the burdens under which the heterosexual couple labour have already gone from the gay couple's lives: they are not legally bound together; they are not tied down by children. The two most pressing of the heterosexual responsibilities need never exist for a gay man or woman. Of course, this should not be read as an endorsement of complete irresponsibility. But the gay man or woman is in a better position – in my way of thinking – to define his or her areas of responsibility.

The truism that we find our partners from within the social circles in which we move is probably more particularly apt for individuals in the gay world. Thus the chances are that two men or women beginning a relationship will already possess friends and acquaintances in common. Though this may be true too for a heterosexual couple, it also seems probable that in a straight relationship the man's friendships will have been with a male peer group and the woman's with a female peer group and that subtle resentments will exist from within both groups against the 'intruder' who has removed the friend from the charmed circle. Remembering the previously stated contention that marriage is destructive of involvements outside the legal relationship, then it can be proposed that the heterosexual couples are *less* likely to form, foster and nurture *new* friendships.

Personal observation has brought me to the conclusion that heterosexual relationships tend to end with far more acrimony than is common with the ending of (male) gay relationships. Straight couples of my acquaintance whose coupledom has collapsed have tended to do so with an incredibly high level of hostility towards each other. Friends are expected to take sides – and if they try to remain on amicable terms with both partners, both will accuse them of disloyalty. Rarely is social contact between partners maintained after separation or divorce – whatever has gone before is ruthlessly destroyed and the man or woman finds themselves (in effect) starting out again from scratch. A new partner has to be found and a completely new set of domestic circumstances created.

Of course, gay relationships can founder and end with an equal amount of loathing. But the chances are that if the two partners came from within a restricted social group in the first place, they will continue as a part of that group and the co-incidence of their meetings will ensure that some kind of (grudging?) friendship will survive. In fact the very nature of gay relationships suggests to me that the continuance of friendships within and outside that relationship will ensure that neither partner suffers from the same numbing sense of post-separation (or death) isolation that can prove so crippling for distanced heterosexual partners. To my way of thinking, the element of sociability that characterises at least some gay partnerships means that gay men and women develop a network of sustaining friendships that can cushion the most shattering blows.

There is a wonderfully apposite little scene in Larry Kramer's novel *Faggots*; Fred Lemish, the protagonist, is discussing with his best friend his need for and the kind of lover he wants. The conversation – and the relevant point – hinges on mention of Anthony's lover. '"Sprinkle isn't much of a kisser," Fred said referring to Anthony's lover, whom Fred, naturally, didn't like or think good enough for his best friend.'

And curiously, one's closest friends always do express some kind of chagrin when they hear that you have fallen in love. But in all probability they will have been through it all before, will have been through the same situation themselves on more than one occasion, and be on hand to share the good times and console if there are bad times.

Ultimately, because the gay couple do not automatically have the support of natural family, they seem more likely to create their own version of a family unit – a family not imposed by birth and blood ties (people you may actively dislike) but chosen because of shared attitudes and affinities. Because the gay couple are less likely to retreat into a mutually self-absorbed exile from friends, the chances are that *they* – and not the heterosexual counterparts – will have a safety net of friendship to coset them when things go wrong. In Robin Swado's Aids play *A Quiet End*, the three central characters – dying together – appeared to be without friends. This was a weakness for it seemed improbable. For in these Aids days we need to look to our friends and lovers and know they – or we – are there when we need them. If – as has been proposed in these pages – gay couples form more sustaining networks of friendship than heterosexual couples, then it is we – and not they – who have more to look forward to in the years to come.

GAY TIMES July 1986

ROCK HUDSON.
THE FULL STORY?

`As for 1985, it took more than non-yellow journalism to ease society through to the next stage in its understanding, its confrontation with Aids,' comments Martin Amis in a postscript to his *Observer* essay 'Double Jeopardy: Making sense of Aids', reprinted in *The Moronic Inferno and Other Visits to America*. 'It took Rock Hudson, a figure with the necessary TV-and-tabloid constituency, someone whose face we had known all our lives.' In effect Aids needed a martyr, someone with a high publicity profile, known to millions who could stand as a symbol which would show the world at large that the Aids virus was no respecter of class, position, race or gender. Rather like Oscar Wilde, Hudson's martyrdom was not self-imposed: circumstances and the tabloid press dictated his role. There can be no doubt that had the actor not contracted Aids, the general public would still be none-the-wiser about Hudson's sexual predilections. "He's a sort of old-world fag," says one of the characters in Armistead Maupin's *Further Tales Of The City*, describing ———, an actor modelled by Maupin (a friend of Hudson's) on Rock Hudson. "I don't understand that," —— says to hero Michael Tolliver, who is shortly to begin a nine city tour with The Gay Men's Chorus. "What?" Tolliver asks. "Why some people make such a big deal out of being gay." The line may belong to a fictional character; the voice seems authentically Hudson.

Four weeks before his death on October 2nd 1985, writer Sara Davidson met Hudson for the first time. It had been agreed that she – in collaboration with the ailing actor – should pen his 'autobiography'. "So much bullshit has been written about me," he told Davidson. "It's time to tell my story. It's time to set things straight." But everyone involved with this venture realised that time was running out. 'We had understood that Rock might not be able to give me the time generally required to write a book about one's life,' she explains in her introduction to *Rock Hudson:*

His Story by Rock Hudson and Sara Davidson. Her time with Hudson was probably even more restricted than either had anticipated – thus the actor's comments on his life and career are sparse and there is little here to indicate that had he survived longer he would have been more frankly forthcoming with Davidson. What the writer managed – and it must have been vitally necessary if she was to complete the book – is to talk to many of the people closest to the movie star. 'Before he died, Rock signed a letter asking his friends to cooperate with me, to tell the truth, the 'whole story',' she continues. 'For many, this was a strange and difficult request. Rock had trained his friends to observe 'total silence', especially with writers. Anyone admitted to the inner circle was told: never speak about what happens at the Castle to the press. Those who broke this rule were dropped.

`Why, now, was Rock releasing his friends? Many agonized about being interviewed. Had Rock been in his right mind? Did he know what he was doing? Should they reveal things that Rock had never publicly admitted during his lifetime?

`Some decided not to participate, but the majority I contacted agreed to talk. It was Rock's wish, and Rock was Master. He had stayed up on the high wire for four decades. He had remained a fixed star in a galaxy where new stars rose and fell each season, and he was going to stay fixed and visible for some time after his passing.'

Amongst those who spoke with Davidson were George Nader and his long-time lover Mark Miller ("Both of us were brought up to believe you fall in love and stay in love for life," says Nader of a relationship that has lasted for thirty-five years). Formerly an actor, ill-health forced Nader to give up his career and now he is better known as a writer, primarily for his slightly fascistic gay science fiction romance *Chrome*; Miller, who trained as an opera singer, was Hudson's personal secretary. These two patently devoted men were close to Rock Hudson almost from the moment he arrived in Hollywood – and theirs is a major contribution to the book. Others interviewed by

Davidson include Tom Clark, Hudson's lover for a decade, who was re-united with his lover after he had contracted Aids; Marc Christian, a villain of the piece (if there is one), Hudson's final live-in lover who, after the star's death, sued the estate and various named and unnamed individuals because (he claimed) they had conspired to endanger his life by *not* informing him of the actor's illness (he discovered the truth after the story made headlines around the world). Phyllis Gates, an assistant to Hudson's first agent, briefly married to the actor between 1955 – 58 (*not* his secretary, as Patricia Bosworth claims in her biography of Montgomery Clift) is still bitter about a marriage that *may* have been of convenience and which certainly quickly soured. She characterises Hudson as a cruel man – though it is more likely that he couldn't cope with a situation that had been forced on him by his Hollywood studio and the gossip and fan magazines. It is the testimony of these – and others – which give the book its substance. And yet the real Rock Hudson remains remarkably elusive.

Born Roy Scherer on November 17th 1925 in Winnetka, Illinois (the heartland of Middle America), Rock Hudson was as much an invention of the Hollywood dream factory as a female star like Lana Turner. His career in movies was firmly rooted in his physical appearance – a rugged and towering idealisation of American manhood, suitably masculine to appeal to male audience, agreeably vulnerable to capture female movie-goers. For years Hudson was Number One box office star – yet a lingering look over his film credits barely reveals a good movie, let alone a great one. He thought his best films were *"Giant, Seconds, Pillow Talk, Lover Come Back. I love* the comedies." he told Davidson. "I got to learn from Doris . . . talk about knowing your craft."

Doris Day was but one of the women who starred with Hudson who became a close friend. "I had never met Rock Hudson before," she says in *Doris: Her Story*, "but the very first day I was on the set I discovered we had a performing rapport that was remarkable. We played our scenes

99

together as if we had once lived them. Every day the set was a picnic – sometimes too much of a picnic, in that we took turns at breaking each other up."

And it was with Doris Day that Rock Hudson gave his last performance – as the guest star in the first of her new television series *Doris Day's Best Friends*.

Elizabeth Taylor, with whom he had co-starred in *Giant*, also became a close friend (though its hard to discover this from the book). According to Michael Wilding in his autobiography *Apple Sauce*, it was Hudson who discovered Montgomery Clift's smashed car after a dinner party at his (Wilding's) and Taylor's home in May 1956. In Bosworth's *Montgomery Clift*, she states that it was actor Kevin McCarthy who found the wreck, but points out it was Hudson in conjunction with the doctor who got the injured actor out of the wreckage. It is one of the noticeable features of *Rock Hudson: His Story*, that there is little indication that Hudson had a Hollywood lifestyle. James Dean – another co-star in *Giant* – barely rates a mention and the reader has to go elsewhere to discover: 'The mutual contempt Jimmy and Rock Hudson held for each other was not far from the on-camera hostility between Jett and Bick. Jimmy had little respect for Hudson's wooden acting, and Hudson resented Jimmy's sullen attitude. They had the bad luck of having to share a house. Some fifteen years later, Hudson admitted to the *Hollywood Reporter* that he didn't particularly like Dean:

`"He and I and Chill Willis lived in a rented house together for three months while we were doing *Giant* in Texas, and although we went more or less our own ways, Dean was hard to be around.

`"He hated George Stevens, didn't think he was a good director, and he was always angry and full of contempt."

`Dean, of course,' continues David Dalton in *James Dean: The Mutant King*, 'was never groomed nor bent as a locker room personality, but Hudson still recalls that Dean "never smiled. He was sulky, and he had no manners. I'm not concerned with manners – I'll take them where I find them – but Dean didn't have 'em.

`"And he was rough to do a scene with for reasons that only an actor can appreciate. While doing a scene, in the giving and taking, he was just a taker. He would suck everything and never give back."'

And if the Hollywood life style is in shadow, what about the Hollywood *gay* life style. Presumably Hudson must have known others from the movie community who shared his sexual inclinations. Did they not socialise? Did he not know people like Sal Mineo (also in *Giant*), Laughton or Cukor (perhaps theirs was too intellectual an ambience), what was his view on someone like Clift? (not even mentioned in the book). Maybe Hudson wasn't 'Hollywood' – a suggestion that is made by Noel Coward, quoted in Cole Lesley's *Life Of Noel Coward*: "All of this surprised the Rock Hudsons," he says, describing an outrageous but sophisticated party, "who are perhaps unused to high society . . . "

Certainly, as the years rolled by, Hudson began to resist the constraints of being so rigidly 'in the closet'. Along with author Armistead Maupin he cruised the bars in the Castro area of San Francisco. He took to visiting Los Angeles gay clubs, and when he was appearing in London at the Phoenix Theatre in the musical *I do, I do*, he made at least one visit to Bang Disco.

Inevitably a very large proportion of *Rock Hudson : His Story* is taken up with Aids (84 of the narrative 234 pages, well over a third of the whole book). It is for this the book will be bought and read and it is this part of the story which is most compelling – sometimes as macabrely funny as a play by Joe Orton, frequently as labyrinthine as a plot by Machiavelli, ultimately intensely moving as the full horror of encroaching death takes over the final section. Holy-rollers speaking in tongues, prayer vigils lead by Mrs Pat Boone, medical treatment – no miracle was forthcoming. And no indignity was spared . . .

Rock Hudson died on October 2nd 1985, at home in his own bed; the press were besieging the house: vultures awaiting the final carrion. The body is placed in a van which is to take it to the crematorium.

`"We can't lock it," the driver said.

`Tom bolted to the door, grabbed the handles and held them closed. He rode all the way to the crematorium on his knees, clutching the doors, straddling Rock's body.

`When they reached the crematorium, the gates were locked to keep out the press. Tom and the driver put Rock on a gurney and carried him into the building where there was a cardboard box that said ROCK HUDSON. They put him in the box, put the box on the gurney and rolled it in the oven. "I saw the box catch fire. I stood watching it; then they closed the oven and I left," Tom says. "It was the hardest thing I ever had to do, but I did it and there weren't any photographs taken."'

As in almost every press story about Aids, *Rock Hudson: His Story* shows the media in an appalling light. Perhaps this compelling but far from satisfactory book will serve as a kind of antidote to the yellow-press hysteria briefly alluded to by martin Amis at the beginning of this piece. Maybe that's a vain hope . . .

All Rock Hudson's earnings from this book go to the Rock Hudson Aids Research Foundation.

GAY TIMES August 1986

ACROSS THE GREAT DIVIDE

"You've betrayed your roots," insisted a friend particularly jealous of his working-class origins and really rather appalled that my conversation was not that of an archetypal cockney, sentences punctuated by cries of 'Gor, blimey', aitches dropped with impunity. That I'd never possessed an East End accent was quite beside the point; to him I had gone through a totally despicable process of gentrification that he viewed as a denial of the background he had so fondly imagined for me.

Yet though never a cockney sparrer, I *had* come from an essentially working-class background and like so many before me had realised that there was another world out there – if not necessarily better then at least considerably more interesting.

In my youth I had been in the position of an acolyte, learning from older gay men about the things that subsequently came to be essential components of my life and personality. Of course, sex came into it – but far more important were literature, music, theatre, films, travel, food and a certain erratic sense of style. I was following in an honourable tradition of what amounted to patronage of working-class youth by middle, upper or intellectual class paternalists ("I've always fallen in love with someone far younger than myself," Robin Maugham told me during an interview. "And now, my relationship is far more – I take far more the position of an incestuous father figure.")

If one wished to be especially pedantic, this cross-generational, cross-class relationship could be traced back to classical Greece – but perhaps it's most interesting manifestation took place between 1898 and 1940 (though it quite clearly stretches for some years on either side of those dates). For example, there are those who have concluded (with a great deal of justification) that Wilde's 'crime' was not his homosexuality but rather his crossing the great British divide of class by socialising with the lower orders. The autobiographical and biographical literature of the period is replete with accounts of relationships – usually (though not invariably) mutually beneficial – between middle-class and upper-class intellectuals and working-class youths. There were undoubtedly many such relationships which existed between perfectly anonymous partners – but these because of their very nature have gone unrecorded. It is also a loss to gay cultural history that those under patronage were not in a position to document *their* view of things. Thus the posthumous appearance of Harry Daley's *This Small Cloud* is to be particularly welcomed.

Born in Lowestoft in 1901, Harry Daley's family was staunchly and respectably working-class: his father, a fisherman, was lost at sea in 1911. One of a closely-knit family of five children (two sisters, two brothers), Daley was clearly a lively and intelligent child – moving by way of Arthur Mee's *Children's Encyclopedia* to adventure stories such as *The Coral Island* and *Mr Midshipman Easy* and the classics: 'Quite soon we were reading Dickens.' Literature, that blissful refuge for the slightly introverted child, was early in evidence in his life.

`I also learnt, enjoyed and remembered romantic items about people like Canute, Rufus and King Alfred; and about burnt cakes, arrows through eyes, spiders going up and down, and Black Princes and Kings who never smiled again,' he writes, retrospectively showing an interest in men of action. 'I was too nervous to play team games and, traditionally for my kind, never succeeded in getting near the ball in one game of football.'

Aware of his attraction to men (specifically what he would term 'masculine' men) from an early age, this statement indicates the thinking evident in gay men of Daley's (and later) generation which posited the view that homosexual men were less than men (an attitude that is given its greatest expression by Quentin Crisp, notably in *The Naked Civil Servant*).

After leaving school, Daley found work as a post office telegraph boy and continued his innocent sexual explorations. During the First World War, the family moved to Dorking, where Daley worked as a grocery delivery boy (amongst the homes to which he undoubtedly delivered was West Hackhurst, residence of E M Forster and his mother – the former of whom was to play an important part in his later life).

Daley left Dorking in 1925, joining the Metropolitan Police. Stationed as a constable in Hammersmith, he made the acquaintance of J R Ackerley. 'They met casually in the street early one Sunday morning," writes P N Furbank in his introduction to *This Small Cloud*, 'and by a pleasant chance it turned out in conversation that Daley, who was an indefatigable theatregoer, had seen a production of Ackerley's play *The Prisoner of War* at the Lyric, Hammersmith. It initiated a long, indeed a lifelong, friendship, and quite soon, through Ackerley, Harry had become friendly with quite a number of Ackerley's literary and artistic acquaintances, amongst them Raymond Mortimer, Duncan Grant, Gerald Heard, Leo Charlton and E M Forster.'

With Forster Daley had an affair which, says Furbank, was 'from a sexual point of view more important to Forster than to Daley, who, though homosexual, was only physically attracted to heterosexuals.' To the likes of Wilde, Edward Carpenter, Ackerley and Forster (and no doubt W Somerset and Robin Maugham, Christopher Isherwood, W H Auden and John Lehmann), working-class men seemed to possess some kind of mythic quality – something ill-defined and almost impossible to pinpoint exactly, but surely a combination of their belonging to the labouring classes making them more manly and manliness being equated with sexual potency.

For the self-improvers (Furbank describes Harry Daley as 'a born self-improver'), the gains from their association with the literati were emotional rather than physical and there can be little doubt that his relationship with men like Forster and the intellectual encouragement they gave him helped refine the fluid literary style used to such effect in this autobiography.

Alas, patronage often causes resentments – with one side suspecting advantage being taken and the other believing that they are viewed as little more than an amusement.

Daley and Forster fell out – somewhat acrimoniously – and were not to meet again until 1960, 'when Ackerley won the W H Smith award and invited Harry to the celebratory dinner at the Savoy. The encounter went very amicably,' Furbank informs us. 'Daley told Forster that he was writing his memoirs but Forster was not to worry, for he had become discreet in his old age. Forster replied genially that he had become *in*discreet in his old age, so Harry could write what he pleased.'

But though Daley *did* write what he pleased, *This Small Cloud* does not detail Daley's relationships and friendships with the great and famous. More interestingly, this is a book about the life as a working man – in that most peculiar of positions, working-class, gay and a policeman. Clearly in his more youthful days Daley was far from discreet and the book is most illuminating about the prejudices he confronted from his colleagues because he was a gay man who did little if nothing to disguise his sexual preferences.

As already mentioned, Daley's interest was in hetero-sexual men, usually older and stronger than himself. A Freudian might suggest that he was searching for a replacement for the beloved father he lost when still a child. Certainly there must at times have been a conflict of loyalties – because Daley seems to have been half in love with the criminal classes he was destined to prosecute. Exactly as Forster and Ackerley viewed the working-class Daley as an ideal of masculinity, so Daley himself looked towards the predominantly heterosexual criminals as an ideal of maleness.

Yet though, undoubtedly physically attracted to the criminals he encountered, Daley was also deeply sympathetic to the working-class men and women (often victims of the Depression) he met in the course of his work. He acknowledges himself a champion of the underdog and the oppressed. In this respect, *This Small Cloud* presents an heart-warming portrait of the old-fashioned bobby on the beat, close kin to Dixon of Dock Green, rather than the harassed and computerised policemen we know today.

Daley's ruthless self-improvement obviously enriched his life and without it is unlikely he would have been able to contemplate let alone complete a volume of memoirs. In effect, Daley's self-improvement led directly to the writing of this rare record of working-class gay experience. There are few – if any – documents of the period to compare (although oral records exist: Jack Hewitt, for example, interviewed by Barrie Penrose and Simon Freeman about his life with Blunt and Burgess for the same author's *Conspiracy Of Silence*; Alan Searle interviewed by Patrick O'Higgins for Morgan's monumental biography of Somerset Maugham).

But the tradition of patronage can now be viewed as a thing of the recent but now historic past. That burning need for self-improvement started to disappear as educational opportunities improved and when – during the Sixties – the rigid social structure *appeared* to be levelled. Yet as our lives change in the ever more divisive Eighties, as hard-won opportunities begin to disappear, will the need for patronage – after all, only a means of sharing – by older gay men of younger return?

It might be no bad thing. For although the very word 'patronage' tends to make us think of people who are 'patronising'; at its best patronage was about sharing and opportunity and, most importantly, communication. There may have been a lot wrong with a system which was basically based on sexual attraction on one side and advancement by means of fulfilling the desires of that attraction, but there can still be little doubt that the self-improvers and their patrons derived mutual benefits from happy relationships. Perhaps today that kind of communication across the great divide of age and class is needed again.

GAY TIMES February 1987

ANDY WARHOL LOOKS A SCREAM

`An artist is somebody who produces things that people don't need to have but that he – for *some* reason – thinks it would be a good idea to give them,' announced Andy Warhol in *From A to B and Back Again: The Philosophy of Andy Warhol* (1975). It was but one of many memorably cynical aphorisms (presumably) coined by one of the late Twentieth Century's most influential painters. Yet Warhol, who died in New York on February 22nd, aged 59, was much more than a pop artist; he was a public figure who put his stamp on a generation, inspiring devotion and derision in just about equal amounts, successfully propelling his image into the public consciousness and turning his name into something best described as a 'brand' name.

"Everybody knows I'm a queen . . . ," Warhol, a man usually so reticent with the press as to make him a rival to Jonson's Epicoene, told Fiona Russel Powell in an interview which appeared in *The Face* in March 1985. Perhaps that was one of the most amazing things about Warhol (born Andrew Warhola on August 8th 1927, of Czech immigrant parents): he shook his homosexuality in the face of the American public and many of them loved him for it. More – he turned the generally socially unacceptable (hustlers, transvestites, transsexuals) into the unattainable by making the likes of Udo Keir, Joe Dallesandro, Jackie Curtis, Holly Woodlawn and Candy Darling into movie stars.

Warhol burst upon the American cultural scene in the early Sixties, gaining fame and fortune for his paintings and silk screen reproductions of such unlikely domestic artifacts as cans of Campbell's soup. This was fine art become fun art and the riches he reaped enabled him to move into film production (including *Sleep, Empire, My Hustler, Lonesome Cowboys, Blue Movie, Flesh, Trash Heat, Andy Warhol's Dracula, Andy Warhol's Bad* – the last half-dozen of which were directed by Paul Morrissey), pop music (Andy Warhol's Velvet Underground) and magazine publishing (*Interview*). As Andrew Katz points out in his *International Film Encyclopaedia*: 'Death and sex have been recurrent themes in Warhol's films. Sexuality has been explicit, spanning the gamut of human experience, with no visible boundaries between heterosexuals homosexual, bisexual, transsexual, and androgynous identities and activities. The exhibition of these films in art theatres helped accelerate the trend towards legitimizing explicit sex on the American screen.' The Warhol movies also – it should be added – helped legitimize the explicit depiction of sex on British screens.

But it was perhaps through his involvement with Velvet Underground that Warhol influenced the most people. From Velvet Underground (and vocalist Lou Reed) can be traced the visual, lyrical and musical styles which percolated across the Atlantic (strongly influencing David Bowie, whose 1971 album Hunky Dory includes a track called 'Andy Warhol' – with the witty and perceptive line 'Andy Warhol looks a scream/Hang him on my wall/Andy Warhol, Silver Screen/Can't tell them apart at all') and then back again. It was Bowie who revitalised Reed's moribund career when he produced the watershed album *Transformer* (which includes the influential anthem *Walk on the Wild Side*, a homage to what by now had become known as Andy Warhol's Factory). Himself a chronic fan ('A good reason to be famous . . . is so you can read all the big magazines and know everybody in all the stories.'), Warhol was courted by admirers in the music business until the end (David Sylvian's 'look' must have been in part inspired by that of Warhol). And the effect Warhol had on at least two generations of musicians travelled downwards from idols to admirers.

An inveterate party and night clubgoer, Warhol obsessively chronicled New York's fashionable society with both his polaroid camera (*Andy Warhol's Exposures*, 1979) and his cassette recorder (*Interview* features interviews of such banality, with every 'um' or 'er' faithfully transcribed,

110

that ultimately, they reduced the subjects from 'stars' to individuals no more interesting and certainly no more articulate than the average Joe on the street).

A survivor of an assassination attempt in 1968 and of steady drug consumption (though in recent years he had become a health and fitness fanatic), Andy Warhol was not destined to make old bones. And the legend itself would have been spoiled (perhaps) had he died an old man in twenty years time. His most famous dictum in the Sixties was oft quoted 'In the future everyone will be famous for fifteen minutes' (turned around in 1979 to 'In fifteen minutes everybody will be famous.'). Warhol's personal fifteen minutes stretched to more than half a lifetime. His fame was well deserved.

GAY TIMES April 1987

HE'S SO FINE

There was an expression current in the Sixties which claimed that without homosexuals, Jews and Australians there would have been no West End theatre. It does not seem inappropriate to adopt the adage and declare that without the blacks and gays popular music would not exist – certainly not in the form we acknowledge today.

There has always been a remarkably strong link between black music and (primarily) gay men. It can be traced back for more than sixty years. In America in the Twenties and Thirties, Harlem was a stomping ground for gay men and – presumably – lesbians who were attracted in part, no doubt, by blues singers Bessie Smith, Ma Rainey and Billie Holiday, whose sexuality inclined them towards women and whose usually male-written lyrics of anguished love affairs would have had a special resonance for the kind of gay men who populated the pages of Blair Niles's 1931 novel *Strange Brother* and stand at the periphery of books by Carl Van Vetchen. White torch singers, Ruth Etting, Helen Morgan, Libby Holman, represented a somewhat toned down version of the blues singers – and their versions of songs in which they literally carried a torch for a man who treated 'em wrong, were (and have remained) equally popular with gay men. The presence in the charts of two albums by Elkie Brooks attests to the enduring appeal of the torch singer and the torch song.

The adoption of black music by gay men was possibly an almost sub-conscious identification with a minority group who were identifiable simply because of their colour and a musical form born of oppression. It would undoubtedly be stretching credibility too far to suggest that there was (or is) any form of total identification – for though the musical may have been acceptable and the individuals performing it objectified as sexual beings, there was much prejudice mixed with the patronage (Van Vetchen, Nancy Cunard, and – in a later period – Colin MacInnes often sound incredibly patronising.)

Yet unless a gay man or a lesbian makes an emphatic statement of sexuality (Quentin Crisp, for example, with his hennaed hair and fine patina of make-up; Radclyffe Hall, with her cropped hair and collar-and-tie) then they are not instantly recognisable as members of a minority group. As a means of self-definition, it may be necessary to adopt certain 'characteristics' which more immediately identify them with *other* groups who are outside social orthodoxy. Interestingly, at much the same time, there had been a notable strain of *Jewish* blues singers, Sophie Tucker, Libby Holman, which suggests that these refugees – predominantly from Eastern Europe and Russia – found something strong with which to identify in the music of the but recently disenfranchised slaves. The cross-fertilisation of African rhythms and Christian belief to be found in spirituals (the roots of blues) harks back to Psalm 137 ("By the rivers of Babylon, there we sat down, yea, we wept when we remembered Zion . . . ") which relates very directly to historical slavery and exile from a remembered homeland. It is perhaps not too far-fetched to intimate that generations of gay men and lesbians have felt themselves in a kind of exile *even in the land of their birth.*

Another point worth making concerns the nature of language used in the lyrics to songs created by black artists. From Bessie Smith to the disco divas who came into prominence with Hi-Energy, the words they sang were more explicitly sexual than those written by the Tin Pan Alley tunesmiths who were producing moon`n'June songs for mass consumption, behind which was the implicit message that romance was white, heterosexual, innocent (brides went to the altar virgins) and essentially the foundation of family life. Black music frankly acknowledges the sexual impulse (Sippie Wallace's 'I'm a Mighty Tight Woman', 1922; Bessie Smith's 'I've Got What It Takes (But It Breaks My Heart to Give It Away)', 1929; to Donna Summer's 'Love To Love You Baby', 1975; and Miquel Brown's classic-gay anthem 'So Many Men, So Little Time',1983). This was music about pleasure (gin and 'it') and pain (faithless lovers) rather than about duty (the beckoning, threatening preacher who stood outside the bedroom door and had to be appeased – with marriage – before desire could be assuaged). Of course, it was all wildly phallocentric – concentrating on men's 'taming' of wild female victims, but that in itself must have had a strong sub-conscious appeal to the duality of gay male sexual experience.

This more-or-less blatant sexuality was of course seen as intensely threatening; sex as pleasure was interpreted as deeply subversive, a denial of the sanctity of family life and thus an attack on the very foundations of Western society. Obviously gay men and lesbians, living on the whole outside the nuclear family structure, could identify with and appreciate this music.

Naturally, there is also a far more simplistic way of explaining this superficial inter-reaction between two cultures: gay men's adoption of black music may just have been (and continues to be) a conscious act of aesthetic rebellion against an entertainment orthodoxy, a means (metaphorically speaking) of sticking two fingers at the mass who oppressively controlled entertainment and thereby imposed *their* social ground rules onto groups to whom they did not directly apply.

Black rock 'n' rollers (Little Richard, James Brown) were both overtly sexual and decidedly camp – Little Richard, like Sylvester twenty years later, clearly a gay black man successfully operating in a world dominated by an intensely macho ethos. In a brief Foreword to *Into the Life: A Black Gay Anthology*, Sylvester writes 'Being first black and then gay . . . how it is to be both black and gay during these difficult times'.

Yet though there is an easily identifiable history of gay men adopting black music, it became more clearly apparent only during the past twenty years. In the Sixties – when London was thought to be 'Swingin' and the youth culture capital of the world – black music (soul, blue beat, ska, most essentially Tamla Motown) became the music of the knowing young; gay *and* straight. Here was another identifiable group – predominantly working-class – with a certain disposable income to be spent on creating an identity well removed from that of parents and older brothers and sisters.

Groups like the Crystals (with a white producer, Phil Spector, and white songwriters), with songs like 'He's a Rebel' or the Chiffons with 'He's so Fine (I wanna make him mine)' were singing lyrics about wanting men – and in many instances men who didn't fit the acceptable mould ('He hit me and I was glad . . . '). Gay men certainly didn't (and increasingly don't) fit the socially acceptable mould – and for young gay men in the Sixties there was much with which to identify in these songs.

Throughout the Sixties, Motown was 'gay music' – much as Hi-Energy was to become twenty years later. Songs like the Four Tops' 'Reach Out, I'll be There' and (notably) 'Standing in the Shadows of Love'; Jimmy Ruffin's 'What Becomes of the Broken Hearted' and 'I've Passed This Way Before'; The Isley Brothers' 'This Old Heart of Mine (Been Broke a Thousand Times)'; Marvin Gaye's 'I Heard it Through the Grapevine' or Mary Wells classic – and much re-released – 'My Guy' obviously struck deep chords within the gay youths who frequented clubs such as LeDuce in Soho. And it is probably no exaggeration to suggest that the initial success of Motown in Britain stemmed from the popularity of the records in gay clubs and coffee bars.

By the Seventies (Donna Summer) the targeting of gay men as consumers of and breakers of black music acts had become a noticeable trend. Gloria Gaynor's 'I Will Survive' became a gay anthem (and a drag act standby) and total ambiguity had two major exponents: the 'Masculine' Grace Jones and the 'Feminine' Sylvester; both of whom were gay disco darlings long before they made the crossover to international chart success.

Seventies' disco neatly transformed itself into Eighties' Hi-Energy, mind-numbing but body-stirring dance music ideal for the proliferating epic-sized discotheques. Yet although the major vocalists were black women, they were singing songs tailor-made for gay men ('So Many Men, So

116

Little Time', 'It's Raining Men') and promoting them through personal appearances and performances in gay clubs up and down the country. It was often as much as a year later that gay discotheque dance hits finally made it into the national and international charts.

The harassed Eighties – with blacks, gay men and lesbians even more distanced from the dominant strata of society – the trend is still up. Claims cannot be made for any real solidarity; but the recognition remains as strong as ever.

GAY TIMES April 1987

AMONGST THE ALIENS

1: Brutality in Brighton.
Being queer-bashed more than five years ago was a traumatising experience from which I've never quite recovered. The confidence with which I used to walk the Brighton streets at night disappeared completely on that unforgettable evening and has yet to return. I doubt that confidence will ever reappear as now – after dark – I find the streets distinctly menacing.

Unless it is in connection with work, I rarely venture out in the evening – and if I do it is never unaccompanied. I like transportation from door to door – as even public transport leaves me feeling rather edgy. The idea of going to a pub or club and then walking solitarily home is utterly unthinkable. There seem too many people on the prowl whose main purpose in my perception is intimidation.

Perhaps this is simple paranoia. Perhaps not. My work as a journalist for the gay press and my friends – gay and straight – mean that I have very little contact with ordinary heterosexual society. Because I am so far removed from 'them', I have very little idea of what 'they' are thinking – although irregular readings of the tabloid press do not encourage me to believe that gay men or women have many friends or allies in the community at large.

I have long sensed hostility, more recently I have encountered it face to face.

2: Prejudice in Paguera.
Recently a group of us (seven in total) visited Mallorca for a two week vacation. We ranged in ages from twenty one to fifty two. We were all male, we were all gay. When we arrived, none of us was particularly self-conscious about being gay or being perceived as a gay group. Things quickly changed.

Paguera is a fairly typical Spanish resort town. It doesn't appear to have had a past and we assumed it had sprung fully formed from the minds of a consortium of developers, architects and entrepreneurs. Fringed by a narrow beach, the resort is built around what must once have been an attractive small bay. Now high rise apartments and hotels dominate and the main street consists almost entirely of souvenir shops, 'English' bars (where true Brits congregate to get away from the foreigners) and German *Bierkellers* (where the Germans congregate to avoid the foreigners). All well and good: this was to be a cheap holiday and we weren't expecting paradise.

We'd arrived late and on our first night, tired, hungry and obviously oblivious to the impression we might create with the massed ranks of heterosexuality, we set out to find a meal. "Let's go to the 'International'," said 'Hotspots' columnist Bill Short, "it's where all the expatriates eat."

As this bar/restaurant was at the end of our block, we complied with his suggestion. Admittedly it was late. But the terrace of the 'International' was still full of diners – British, by the look of them. As we trooped up the steps, conversation ceased and everyone present glared. A waiter hurried towards us, announcing "We're closed."

"Didn't you notice the hostility?" I asked as we regained the street.

"Don't take any notice," Bill countered. "He's paranoid."

But it didn't take the others long to realise that for once my feelings were accurate. As someone, somewhere wrote: Even paranoids have enemies. And clearly, in this haven of heterosexuality, seven men of various ages and styles of dress stood out like the proverbial sore thumb. That one of our group (the youngest) could just about have passed as the son of any of the three eldest and that another was a *sportif* black made matters even more confusing for 'them'. It quickly became apparent they 'they' had made the correct assumption about us: that we were gay. It also became rapidly clear that the people around us were not just prejudiced against gays. They patently didn't expect to see (or wish to see) a black man in their Eden. On the beach, in the street, in the shops and restaurants, people unashamedly pointed and stared at Toby.

The hostility was both explicit and implicit. We came to feel like Martians who had landed on Earth and found themselves objects of fear and loathing by the natives: to us, these people were aliens; to them we were aliens. And in a very real sense what we were suffering from was culture shock. At home all seven of us are openly gay and accepted as such by friends from both side of the sexual divide. Thus, to enter a world of rampant and unthinking heterosexuality came as an unpleasant shock.

It also gave us pause for thought – because we suddenly realised that *most* gay men and women encounter this kind of hostility for much of their lives. We conceded that our professions (including student, journalist, clothier, novelist and sports instructor) protected us (to a degree) from the slings and arrows of outraged heterosexuality. In a sense, we were privileged.

We would shop earlier and earlier each day – in what sometimes seemed a vain attempt to avoid the loutish Germans and the loutish British. The former stomped around singing what sounded ominously like Nazi marching songs and giving each other salutes which owed more to Hitler than they did to Chancellor Kohl; the latter serenaded us across the bay with less than rousing choruses of 'Here we go. Here we go" and 'You"ll Never Walk Alone". Though none of us are at all separatist, we longed for some separation from the aliens. Unexpectedly, we found we missed the breath of our own kind. Ultimately we found ourselves retreating to the balcony of our apartment and staying there. That much hostility is daunting (to say the least) and none of us felt inclined to expose ourselves to it more than was absolutely necessary.

At Palma airport, as we awaited our long delayed 'plane home, the seven of us sat in a row facing an even larger row of family groupings. Their faces were set, their eyes glistened with dislike. Behind upraised hands, comments were made. 'They' had no reason to feel this way about 'us' – yet clearly we were seen as something alien (a menace? a threat?) and 'they' could not conceal their loathing. By this time, I must admit, the feeling was reciprocated.

3. Paranoia?

Much as we'd like to believe otherwise, the yammerings of the tabloid press shape people's imaginations (inflame?) and direct the way they think. The constant 'exposing' of people as gay, the ceaseless barrage of misinformation about Aids has nourished the populace-at-large's fear and hatred of homosexuals.

Am I being paranoid?

I no longer know.

Shortly after our return from Mallorca, we encountered three acts which were decidedly hostile – but we weren't sure if they were directed at us.

On a Sunday evening a gang of louts, en route to the local pub, went passed the house shouting 'Cocksuckers'; on the Monday and Thursday of the same week a gang of yobs (the same?) went passed shouting 'Aids carriers. Aids carriers.'

Because we weren't sitting in the window, watching the street, we don't know if these remarks were directed at us. It seems a bit of a coincidence . . . If the remarks were aimed at us, I'm not paranoid; if they weren't, it's dispiriting – but marginally less awful than it could be. Either way, the fact that groups of young men (and other friends have had more direct experiences of this kind) can walk the streets chanting such slogans is frightening. It causes me to pause and wonder where it will end.

I have my own thoughts on that.

Two years ago, writing in *Time Out*, I stated that I could envisage a future in which people were dying because of Aids rather than from it. Maybe it's my own paranoia – but I feel the aliens are closing in and the future I predicted is getting closer.

GAY TIMES September 1987

MEN IN THE KITCHEN

Rick Leed's *Dinner for Two* is possibly the only book on cookery directed at a specifically gay readership and is almost certainly the only book on food to have been originated by a gay publishing house (Gay Sunshine Press,1981). 'My original idea was to write a "how to" cookbook for gay men who never learned to cook but found themselves wanting to cook dinner for a lover, a date, or other guest,' Leed writes in his Introduction. 'In our sex-role oriented society, many men were never encouraged to learn to cook ("A man's place is *not* in the kitchen," etc),' he continues. 'Recently, however, I've become convinced that more and more men have learned or are learning the basics of cookery, at least in part through the recent popularisation of cookbooks. So I decided that my cookbook should be a "dinner for two" cookbook with a gay accent but designed for those with all levels of experience in the kitchen."'

Leed's basic premise (`more and more men have learned or are learning the basics of cooking') is one that no alert or aware individual could disagree with – though in their recent *On Food*, Elizabeth Jane Howard and Fay Maschler include a chapter on men abandoned by their women who have to fend for themselves but who are clearly innocents so far as culinary experience is concerned. Howard and Maschler are of the view that the male in the kitchen can contend with little more demanding than a hamburger – and that even that might try the poor dears' abilities.

Elizabeth Jane Howard and Fay Maschler obviously endorse the maxim earlier dismissed by Leeds – 'A man's place is *not* in the kitchen' – and by doing so deny the evidence that must regularly confront their eyes. For decades the great chefs of the world have been male and for some not inconsiderable time *some* of the great writers on food have been men (Boulestin, Escoffier, Dumas, Brillat-Savarin, Soyer – to name but a handful of the classics). More recently it has been men writing on food who have captured the public imagination – often aided by regular appearances on television (Keith Floyd or Ken Hom, for example).

Of course, the concept of a cookery book 'with a gay accent' is little more than a publishing gimmick. After all, there is no such thing as 'gay food' and what gay men (or women – surely not exclusively using recipes from *The Alice B Toklas Cookbook*?) eat is dictated by taste diet and economics rather than sexual preference (though increased awareness of Aids *may* have caused many of us to opt for healthier eating).

Naturally there are writers who are themselves gay who have written about food – Rupert Croft-Cooke (*Cooking For Pleasure, English Cooking, Exotic Food* etc), Alan Wakeman and Gordon Baskerville's *The Vegan Cookbook*, Norman Douglas's *Venus in the Kitchen*, John Fothergill's waspish *Innkeeper's Diary* trilogy, Desmond Brigg's *Entertaining Single-handed*, several volumes from Roger Baker back in the Seventies and a regular stream of primarily vegetarian cookery books from Colin Spencer spring instantly to mind. But these books are concerned with food and the writer's sexuality does not obtrude (though knowledgeable readers may already hold this information and perceptive readers may guess it).

To know, for example, that Fothergill was a friend of Wilde and a subject of portraitist Romaine Brooks gives a special complexion to his writing. To be aware that Norman Douglas fled Britain 'under a cloud no bigger than a small boy's hand' might cause readers of *Venus In The Kitchen* to view the book with somewhat enhanced perceptions. The knowledge that Roger Baker and Colin Spencer are contributors to the British gay press might cause their writing about food to have resonances for the gay reader which simply would not exist for the straight.

But why do men cook? The obvious response to that is: Why shouldn't they? Men, gay or straight, now take pleasure in the planning, preparation and serving of meals. These are accomplishments which call for imagination and skill and at which only the most crass would sneer or scorn as effeminate. Why should heterosexual men be totally dependent on women in the kitchen? Why should women and not men be *expected* to cook? Many men, gay and straight, simply do not have women at hand to cook for them – and presumably a large number of those men don't want to subsist on a dreary diet of burgers, fish and chips, curry and take-away Chinese. Thus one reason for men cooking stems from basic need.

Once essential cooking skills have been mastered, any cook will become more adventurous. The desire to share the fruits of kitchen labours begins to creep to the fore. And preparing food for others is both an indication of affection (enemies aren't offered dinner) and a means of collecting together friends for a convivial gathering. Thus another reason for cooking is because it fosters friendship (or romance) and is an adjunct to sociability.

There is no reason to believe that gay men are more social than their heterosexual counterparts, but they may be social in different ways. It is perhaps more likely that a number of gay men will gather round a dinner table at which a meal prepared by one (or more) of them is to be served than it is that a gathering of heterosexual men will collect together around a table at which a dinner prepared by one (or more) of them is to be served. From amongst the former grouping, it is likely that a number will have cooking abilities; from amongst the latter group, far less are likely to cook on a regular basis. The former – from necessity – have to possess a degree of self-sufficiency; the latter are perhaps more likely to be involved in a relationship in which the female partner fends for the pair of them. Though in my experience more and more heterosexual couples are dividing the labour – with the male half cooking because he enjoys it (as a creative outlet?) and the female half spurning almost totally the kitchen because she feels no desire to do *a job* traditionally assigned to her sex.

Men who cook are inclined to become enthusiasts and enthusiasm (or passion) is catching; enthusiasts are like missionaries – they are always on the look out for converts. Here – then – is a process of generation which indicates

125

that the number of men in the kitchen will steadily increase and multiply. And if men venture no further into the kitchen than the kitchen bookshelf – and browse through a volume by Elizabeth David, Jane Grigson, Alan Davidson or Elizabeth Ayrton – they will be continuing that life enhancing educational process by learning about food values, history, geography, science, economics. Without a doubt, the man (or woman) who is tired of food is tired of life. But who could ever become bored with the riches of the kitchen?

GAY TIMES October 1987

IS IT REALLY PINK?

[acronym *n*. a word formed from the initial letters of a group of words; for example, UNESCO for the *United Nations Educational, scientific, and cultural organisation. Collins English Dictionary*, 1979.]

The world appears to have gone acronym mad. If we swallowed whole everything we encountered in the media, we'd think we lived in a science fiction world populated entirely by WASPS, YUPPIES and DINKIES (or, for the uninitiated, *W*hite *A*nglo-*S*axon *P*rotestants, *Y*oung *U*rban *P*rofessional *P*ersons, and people with *D*ouble *I*ncome *N*o *K*ids). Some acronyms amuse (Harrods can now be interpreted as 'Have another Rolls Royce on daddy, sweetie'); some are the basis for distress (Aids is the most obvious example). Some – if not all – appear to have been invented just to give journalists a snappy headline. All exist as irritating shorthand which allows the writer or broadcaster to identify a given group in a brisk and convenient manner.

We – that is gay men – have now achieved the somewhat dubious distinction of acronymity. If a recent London *Evening Standard Magazine* article is to be believed. We live in a world of MINK. Now that very word 'mink' has certain connotations of riches and idle femininity swathed in expensive furs, so it comes as no surprise to discover that the acronym which so adroitly adopts the name of a fur bearing rodent stands for *M*ale *I*ncome, *N*o *K*ids. Faggots in fact – which to many a prejudiced mind conjures up an image of idle femininity (albeit in a male body) wrapped if not in expensive furs then at least surrounded by expensive possessions.

Yes, the ubiquitous pink pound has resurfaced. This symbol was adopted more than a decade ago by a gay community rejoicing in what appeared to be a burgeoning sub-cultural economy (though never one to compare with that which really *did* flourish in America and because of which lesbians and gay men gained political clout). But

127

certain sections of the British media hijacked the concept of the pink economy, a pink pound and have used it ever since as a covert weapon which tries to convince 'us' and most especially tries to convince 'them' that gay men have a far higher disposable income than most of the rest of the population, that gay men are – in a word – rich.

Within the gay world the concept of pink means one thing; *outside* the gay world it means something entirely different. *Within* it is a symbol of pride – stemming from the pink triangle the Nazis forced (primarily German) homosexuals to wear in the concentration camps, now a logo to be worn with pride, increasingly, one suspects, as a pink badge of courage. *Outside* pink is used as a slur – because of the straight world's association of the colour with femininity and, by implication, softness.

Whoever it was who first hijacked the concept of a pink economy, a pink pound clearly thought they'd lucked in on a good angle for a perennially useful space-filler: the way gay men live (lesbian women are of far less interest within this particular context to the popularist pundits). So the media-at-large's use of the symbolic pink pound has now saddled us with another broad general misconception – that *all* gay men are well-heeled – which, in its own way, is as pernicious as the propagated hysteria about Aids.

Anyone with a passing knowledge of Twentieth Century history will remember that Hitler played upon German disaffection by asserting that the German Jews had all the jobs, all the money. He proclaimed them 'haves' and by so doing implied that the German Jews had dispossessed the non-Jewish Germans, making them into 'have-nots'. He created a focus for resentment. That his argument was errant rubbish then and in any context rubbish now doesn't stop those currently moulding popular opinion from again utilising it.

At best we might believe these journalists are not aware of the sub-text implicit in such statements as 'not only is the gay male couple, living together, the *equal* in potential spending power of the marketing man's dream, the heterosexual dinky – dual income, no kids – pair, but they are arguably superior, because they have two *male* incomes, at a time when women, whatever their aspirations, still earn less than men. What a concept! MINKS – male incomes, no kids – a love of going out, discos, bars, a feel for clothes, furnishings, interiors, holidays. One estimate of the UK gay market was a cool £50 million, and that was three years ago. Think pink? Think Mink!' (Ian Cotton, 'The power of the pink pound', London *Evening Standard Magazine*, January 1988).

Perhaps that all-important sub-text might need spelling out. Claiming that a minority possesses something the majority craves (a high disposable income) sets up an envy syndrome and – within this kind of context – that envy syndrome encourages the 'have nots' (here our heterosexual majority) to ponder ways by which they can revenge themselves on the 'haves' (here a homosexual minority) by removing from them the object of desire: this imagined wealth.

But what this kind of attitude doesn't take into account (and this is pre-supposing that the journalists involved are simply unthinking rather than subtly malicious) is that by proposing a group of people as more affluent, more able to enjoy their leisure time, more glamorous, sets up festering resentments which can only bode ill for what is useful to refer to as the gay community. At worst, of course, such journalists know *exactly* what they are doing and quite deliberately set out to foster prejudice and hatred.

Clearly whoever invented the pink pound had no idea that their journalistic shorthand would become a weapon in the hand of bigots. Equally, however, the originator only had in mind the visible tip of the gay male iceberg – those who did/do have a certain amount of money to spend on leisure activities – and not the higher proportion of gay men who have financial pressures more-or-less identical to their heterosexual counterparts. Thank God that for every Ian Cotton there is a Polly Toynbee who can acknowledge that 'homosexuals are not an identifiable economic group, no richer nor poorer than the rest of us' ('Freedom's roadblock', *The Guardian*, Jan 14, 1988). But unfortunately

Ms Toynbee will have far less effect than Mr Cotton.

Of course, there *are* rich gay men. Equally there are rich heterosexual men. There are certainly large numbers of gay men who live in comfortable circumstances. Equally there are vast numbers of heterosexual man who live in comfortable circumstances. There are also growing numbers of dispossessed of either sexual inclination. That gay male automatically equates with wealth is a ridiculous – and dangerous – idea; the ludicrous journalistic concept of MINK should be stamped out as soon as possible.

Most of 'us' are no more 'haves' than most of 'them' – to allow this belief to prosper allows a prejudice to flourish in an area which affects us all: economics. It's a vain hope, but if only the Cottons of this world would discover that so far as the pound in our pockets is concerned we're no better off than anyone else.

GAY TIMES March 1988

WHO DOES THE DISHES?

All relationships are unequal. Some relationships are more unequal than others. No two people – whatever the gender combination – establishing themselves as a pair under a shared roof (friends *or* lovers) can even begin to hope for a perfect balance. Causing the scales to tip unevenly one way or another are a whole series of considerations – ability, intellect, levels of sexual desire, financial capabilities, areas of interest, age, class, energy or the lack of it amongst them. And who does the dishes?

Until women took a stand against being classed as and treated as domestic and sexual servants, the relationship between a male/female couple at least had recognizable demarcation lines. *He* was the 'breadwinner', she was the 'homemaker'. To a certain degree, that's slowly changing – though a high proportion of men remain undomesticated (*domestically unaware*) and a high proportion of women still see themselves fulfilling a traditional 'caring' role.

But where are the demarcation lines in a same-sex relationship? Most especially, where are the demarcation lines in a male to male relationship – be it between two men living together as a couple or two (or more) men living together from either convenience or because of compatibility? Who does the dishes?

In heterosexual terms, many men (*still*) leave the care of their mothers only when they marry (or set up home with a woman who is wife in all but name) and move into the care of a woman who is destined (doomed?) to continue in the role of mother. Thus, some heterosexual men can go through the entire process of living without ever having to fend for themselves.

However loving they may be, these are often the men who are domestically unaware – those who believe that what happens in a house happens as if by magic: meals prepare themselves, bedroom drawers constantly refill themselves with clean shirts and underwear, floors scrub themselves. No human effort is entailed. This is not wilful unwillingness on their part; it is almost total obliviousness. Some men simply have no concept of what it takes to keep a home running . . .

Now, what happens when two (or more) domestically unaware *gay* men set up house together?

Perhaps one of the more popular (but most irritating) misconceptions about gay men is that they are inherently domesticated – a belief that stems, of course, from the totally inaccurate view that gay men are really ersatz women. It is presumed that by some curious kind of osmosis, gay men grow up with the domestic attributes actually 'bred' into women. But gay men are – first and foremost – men and, therefore, 'breadwinners'.

So here we have an imagined (not so imagined) household of gay men – neither (or none) of whom has grown up anticipating life as a domestic drudge and one (or more) of whom will prove completely incapable. All men are curiously proud of their masculinity (whatever that is), so possess an in-built prejudice against feminizing themselves by becoming domestic. "I can't do much as boil an egg" is a proud boast and *not* an admission of incompetence.

Gay men creating a domestic establishment are not – or should not be – aping a heterosexual menage; role-playing in male to male relationships *appears* to have largely disappeared (and along with it those offensive labels 'butch and bitch', 'active and passive' which did try to define male relationships in terms with which heterosexuals – however remotely – could identify). Thankfully, we *don't* think of gay men as being either 'caring' or 'breadwinners' – perhaps we think of them (us) as being a happy blend of the two.

But any household will contain those who do and those who don't tackle the domestic chores. There can't be anyone who comes home after a hard day at work and actively wants to rinse the smalls or hoover the carpet (male or female) but there are those who realise that these things have to be done and those who – like Quentin Crisp – are willing to let the dust gather because they know that after the first few years it won't get any deeper.

Is this – should this be – a cause for dissent?

An autobiographical note: My cohabitant (amicable not amorous) is a burgeoning politician (and may have been elected to the local council by the time this gets into print). Though undeniably a 'caring' person – forever marching, attending meetings and talking to potential constituents – he is almost the archetypal domestically unaware man. Laundry piles up in his bedroom – until I can't bear it and scoop it out and into the washing machine. Does he know what a vacuum cleaner is? I don't know. Is he aware that the meal he's just eaten *hasn't* come out of Sainsbury's freezer cabinet? Probably not. Is he aware that the rubbish is taken away on Monday morning – and that the sacks have to be heaved out front? Probably not. Does he mean to be so unhelpful? Surely not – but his mind is on higher things. It's far more interesting putting the world to rights than it is putting the house in order. Does he think I'm unreasonable when I ask him to pop down to the corner shop and buy a pint of milk and a loaf of bread? Indeed he does. Do I think he's unreasonable when yet again he fails to accomplish the most simple domestic chore? Indeed I do. But does all this cause conflict?

The simple answer to that is "No" – and for the very basic reason that I've long since worked out that in any same sex grouping there are those who do and those who don't and nothing in the world will change that. Discussions or house meetings about sharing the domestic load may provoke a change of heart – but it will be a brief change of heart and an unwilling change of heart and will be far more likely to cause resentment than *rapprochement*. Down that path is disaster.

He who feels the need to maintain at least a semblance of domestic order should get on with it or give up the experiment and live alone (in which situation *all* chores will fall quite naturally his way). All relationships are unequal; some are more unequal than others – and all are based upon some kind of compromise. Those who bond themselves with undomesticated animals must find some satisfaction in the situation (it's something to complain about) and there must be compensations. There's a lot more to life than doing the dishes.

Ho hum . . . back to the sink!

GAY TIMES June 1988

THE ENEMY WITHIN

`If Roy Marcus Cohn had been merely a cheater, a liar and a thief, a hypocrite, a showoff and a boor, a sexual libertine, a malicious gossip and a bad lawyer, he might have gone through life relatively unnoticed,' commented an American reviewer of Nicholas von Hoffman's *Citizen Cohn*.

`What distinguished him was the scale of what he did, the visibility of it, the self-assured ease with which he would break any rule, manipulate any system, exploit any advantage , besmirch any adversary. Ultimately, by those monumental and on-going excesses, he became a living metaphor for modern-day personal corruption.

`Roy Cohn was a sleaze. He didn't pay his bills, his debts, his taxes or his employees. He betrayed devoted friends, he neglected legal clients, he even ate, regularly and shamelessly, off other people's plates. As a 21-year-old assistant US attorney he fed self-interested tips to columnist Walter Winchell. As the red-baiting chief counsel to Sen. Joseph McCarthy, he destroyed careers of essentially innocent people. As a political fixer, a media manipulator and a high-profile, low-diligence lawyer, Cohn lived his life in the trough of personal indulgence. His excesses ultimately killed him in 1986, a victim of Aids contracted sometime during years of unbridled homosexual profligacy . . . '

In those few succinct words, Gary Blonston seems to have encapsulated Cohn – but if he seems harsh, think again. For Blonston doesn't get around to cataloguing one of Citizen Cohn's most unpleasant characteristics: his violent homphobia.

`At the time millions of homosexual men were stepping forward to press for various kinds of legal protection, Roy worked against them,' acknowledges von Hoffman in his lengthy and detailed portrait. '"I can remember," said one of the people who worked for Roy, "driving him to some outfit, oh, along the lines of The American Society for the Preservation of the Family, quote and unquote, and I drove Roy and his male date to the affair and Roy delivered his address attacking gay rights and then they came out and I drove them to dinner . . . " During the years of debate over the passage of gay rights municipal ordinance in New York, Roy lobbied against the measure and would call up the City Council president's father to ask, "For Christ sakes, what's Andy defending the fags for?" After a judge, acting on a petition from the Roman Catholic Archdiocese of New York, blocked a gay rights measure by the mayor, Roy had judge Alvin Klein as his guest at the Alfred E Smith charity dinner, the biggest, most public annual political do in the city . . . '

Amongst Cohn's confidants was J Edgar Hoover – whom Richard Gid Powers in his recent biography of the FBI chief convincingly propounds was *at least* emotionally homosexual. Another friend was the outré Cardinal Spellman – whose biographer came under pressure from the American Catholic Church to remove all references to the cleric's homosexuality from his book. As is well attested, neither Hoover nor Spellman were friends to the 'friends of Dorothy'.

But lest we lull ourselves into thinking that homophobic homosexuals are either an historical or an exclusively American phenomenon, let me cite an example far closer to home.

In the local elections in May, a Conservative candidate standing in Brighton, until recently owner of a gay guest house and himself gay, was in contact with one of his constituents – who happened to be a *Gay Times* contributor. The burgeoning politician's letters were passed to me – and a careful reading left me slack-jawed with astonishment. For here was a gay man writing in defence of Section 28 (`a needed clause to protect the very people it is meant to pro-tect and they have every right to look to central government for protection when they feel that their local authority is out of order, and not paying them any attention') and endorsing the myths consistently reiterated by the homophobic British press (from *The Sun* to *The Sunday Telegraph*). Can he be serious when he writes 'the gay community (both homosexual and lesbian) is, as a group, probably the most well-off group in the UK. A gay person has more disposable income than any other. If that gay person lives with a partner and expenses are shared, then that makes them even better off financially. Even those gays out of work end up with more disposable income than their counterpart who is heterosexual. The average gay person has no family to maintain and certainly is not the provider for others. There are, of course, one or two exceptions to this rule, but in general what I say is fact'? Of course he's serious . . . But thankfully he was soundly defeated.

No apologies are made for quoting from this distasteful document. Though this political hopeful was happy to have his disgraceful opinions widely aired (`please feel free to quote all or part of this letter. You might consider an article in the form of an interview with me?'); it wasn't my opinion that he warranted serious consideration – not least because it was impossible for me to agree with his view that 'the views expressed here are the views of the great silent majority of gays . . . ' If they are – then God help us, but it seems improbable that most of us (`both homosexual and lesbian') actually support the legislation that oppresses us or agree with the ridiculous theories of Fleet street or Wapping's 'finest'.

Writing about Roy Cohn's days in Washington as McCarthay's right-hand man, Hoffman explains 'For a young, Jewish, homosexual, anti-communist prosecutor these must have been strange, dangerously confusing, and exciting days.' He then goes on to try to rationalise Cohn's homophobia. 'While Roy is remembered as being a part of Washington's gay bar scene, it's not known if Roy thought of himself as homosexual. The definitions of such terms, hardly clear now, were yet foggier in the early 1950's, when even the word "gay" was only beginning to come into use.

`Hence a man had to accept some upsetting labels if he called himself a homosexual. It appears that for Roy the definition of a homosexual was a man with womanish mannerisms. This is apparent in an embarrassed, thick-tongued denial of his sexuality he gave to interviewer Ken Auletta in the 1970's when high school students had come to know that many a gay is anything but a limp-wristed, lavender lad. "Anybody who knows me," said Roy, depending on definitions of a quarter of a century earlier, "and knows anything about me or who knows the way my mind works or the way I function . . . would have an awfully hard time reconciling that with ah, ah, reconciling that with, ah, ah, any kind of homosexuality. Every facet of my personality, of my, ah, aggressiveness, of my toughness, of everything along those lines, is just totally, I suppose, incompatible with anything like that . . . "'

By way of slight mitigation, it is *almost* possible to consider Roy Cohn a victim of his historical environment. Yet the last twenty years of his life were post-Stonewall and should have enabled him to express a degree of self-acceptance and a level of commitment to a cause the betterment of which was directly to his advantage. He remained in the closet to the end – an enemy, wanting only the pleasures and not the politics. A public figure who could have been of use (however dubious an ally), Cohn continued to death a foe of the people he should have been fighting for.

And the Conservative candidate? He comes from the post '67 Sexual Offenses Act generation and *should* be without the self-loathing that is evident from his letter. He has – however – fallen victim of the poison disseminated by the press. Clearly he believes the lies and distortions to be true; worse, clearly he believes he is an inferior being whose lifestyle endangers others. To hold these views is sad – and bad – enough, to wish to spread them from a very public platform makes him another enemy of his people.

Roy Cohn saw advantages in introducing Rupert Murdoch to President Reagan . . .

Need more be said? Draw your own conclusions about the enemies within. Scorn them, spurn them. For in my view they are beneath contempt.

GAY TIMES August 1988

138

COPING WITH THE END

The young Australian doctor who had so infuriated me the day before came into the room where we were waiting and sat down facing us. "I imagine you can guess what I'm going to ask," he said. "We would like to go on using Ian's body in the interest of medical science."

Through the thick layer of grief, I felt anger again.

*****

Two-and-a-half years before his death, Ian McGee was diagnosed as HIV antibody positive. He carried within him what is commonly thought of as the Aids virus. He immediately informed his lover, Alan. A short time later, he notified me. Over the next few months – at what he considered the apposite moment – he told those of his friends who were closest to him. This was a great act of generosity on his part – because much as we like to think that those pronounced Body Positive will survive, at a far deeper level most of us fear they will die within the immediately foreseeable future (though, of course, medical evidence doesn't support this view).

There can be little doubt that Ian believed he was confronting death – even though (as subsequent events proved) he possessed a tenacious will to survive. By telling each of us about the health crisis he faced, he was allowing all of us a time of preparation – for the first signs of illness, for hospitalisation, for his eventual death . . .

*****

I first encountered Ian at a New Year's Eve party in Bayswater as 1965 became 1966. I was nearing twenty-one, he was approaching eighteen. We knew each other as lovers for years, later as fond friends – though for the past dozen years I have been based in Brighton and he in London. We had worked together and played together and – to the end

– were linked by property. At the time of his mother's death in 1985, we had made mutually beneficial wills.

In the months between his diagnosis and his death, I saw no more than was usual with Ian – but (particularly more recently) each time I saw him, I was aware of weight loss and very evident tiredness. On the last occasion he stayed with me in Brighton, he slept through much of the weekend.

✳ ✳ ✳ ✳ ✳

The last time I spoke with Ian before he was hospitalised was in the first week of June. Our conversation was worryingly brief. "I can't stop," he said, "I've got the most awful attack of diarrhoea. I'll phone . . . "

I'd long been aware that Ian was subject to these attacks of diarrhoea. He'd even cut down the amount of orange juice he drank because I'd suggested that too much fruit juice might cause stomach upsets. Now I realise he must have been suffering from opportunistic intestinal infections.

I thought the diarrhoea a worrying symptom, but in all our conversations Ian had never confirmed that he was suffering the first signs of Aids-related illness. Though we had frequently talked about death, we had not discussed illness. Because we weren't the kind of people who had a regular pattern of contact, I wasn't concerned about not hearing from Ian over the next few days.

Early on the morning of Saturday, June 18th, Karen de Groot, a friend for eighteen years, telephoned me. "Darling," she said, "I think you should know that Ian is in St Stephen's Hospital. He's been there since Monday. He didn't want you to know. He knew you'd worry. I've broken a confidence by telling you, but because you're his oldest friend I felt you had to know."

Plans which couldn't be changed had been made for the weekend. More importantly, I knew I needed time to prepare myself. "I'll be up on Monday," I said. "I'd better phone Lisa."

But after replacing the receiver, I didn't immediately call Lisa, Ian's second cousin (to whom he was more like a fond

140

and sometimes indulgent older brother). As on similar occasions in the past, I had a presentiment.

Ian was going to die.

After the initial painful tears, I telephoned Lisa. Ian was suffering from pneumonia (*pneumocystis*) and a parasitic infection of the brain (toxoplasmosis), she told me. He was dehydrated because he had been unable to either eat or drink for the week prior to hospitalisation. He weighed less than six stone, was suffering from impaired vision and was having great difficulty in speaking.

Relentlessly practical, I asked: "Is it terminal?"

"I'm so glad you asked that," Lisa responded. "It's been at the forefront of my mind all week, but I've not dared to articulate it. Yes, I think it is."

*****

It is not my intention to rehearse the brief but painful course of Ian's illness. It is too soon and it would be disturbing. My purpose in writing this is to raise questions and to enumerate experiences that might – by example – be of service to others dealing with similar situations at some point in the future.

*****

During the course of that last weekend with me, Ian and I again discussed death – primarily in connection with our need to revise our wills. We had both been long aware of the importance – especially for gay men and lesbians – of legally binding documents relating to the disposal of property and possessions after death. We had our wills – but in the three years since these had been drawn up our situations had changed. At the time, we were in the midst of negotiations which would change things further.

"Once all this is sorted out, we must make new wills," I said. "You must make sure that Alan's looked after; I'll have to make sure that Hugh's taken care of." Concern about the status of lovers or close co-habitees after one's death should be of prime importance to gay men and women.

"Sure," Ian acknowledged, "but we can't go on talking about this. Life goes on . . . "

As it turned out, Ian didn't have time to revise his will – but fortunately as both main beneficiary and Executor, I was in a position to implement such wishes of his that I was aware of. Had there been no will, Ian's estate would have gone to his nearest of kin . . . a homophobe who could have created heart-breaking problems for Alan and (possibly) myself.

Don't wait until you're ill, don't wait until middle or old age are upon you: make a will now.

✻ ✻ ✻ ✻ ✻

When someone close to us is terminally ill, we almost expect the world to stop in awareness and acknowledgement of our grief. Life isn't like that – though in heterosexual circumstances it *may* happen, in gay circumstances it is less likely to happen. At best, most people simply don't comprehend the bonds that tie same sex couples and – thus – make little or no allowances at times of distress. Life goes on . . .

Therefore – whilst the process of dying is taking place (and in the aftermath of death) – one needs to organise one's real world as completely as possible so as to be able to cope adequately with the unreal world of dying and death. Employers may be unsympathetic, some friends will not be able to confront the situation. These things must be faced and handled. I found that by remaining briskly professional and thinking ahead – what had to be done at work, what could be done for Ian (and friends), what problems might be arising and how to handle them – enabled me to get through each day without the additional pressures from things forgotten, tasks left undone.

✻ ✻ ✻ ✻ ✻

Because for so much of his time in hospital, Ian was in Intensive Therapy the number of visitors he could see was restricted. This meant that there were large numbers of friends who – although they wanted to – could not visit. We (Alan, Lisa and I) decided that it was important that everyone who wanted personal contact should have an opportunity to feel that *they* had done *something* and we suggested that those who couldn't visit send cards or photographs. Even though we suspected that Ian was having difficulty seeing, we knew that nurses or those of us who were visiting would read messages to him. He would not feel neglected or forgotten, neither would those sending the cards or photographs feel excluded. We thought it vital that everyone who wanted some involvement in the process of Ian's dying should participate. *Excluding people at a time like this means that those 'kept out' could feel (at the time and in the future) a residual sense of guilt.*

By sharing grief – and most importantly, talking about it and about Ian – I feel that we somehow eased the anguish.

Occasionally, now, I wonder if we might not have helped kill Ian with kindness. Of course, we didn't – but I have come to believe that we put too much pressure on him by spending too much time with him when we visited. It is important to remember that the patient is almost certain to feel a sense of obligation to his/her visitors – and thus may tire themselves because, in a sense, they are having to 'entertain' their visitors. I am now convinced that shorter visits might have been easier for Ian (most importantly) and for those visiting (because shorter visits would have been less of a strain and less of an emotional drain).

In a sense we were a particularly lucky group – as most of us were articulate and thus able to say what we were thinking, what we were feeling. If we had not been able to use words as a salve in this way, our distress might have been greater.

*****

Ian entered St Stephen's Hospital on June 13th, he spent a week in Thomas Macaulay Ward, was moved into Intensive Therapy on June 20th, operated on June 30th,

143

returned to Thomas Macaulay Ward and died there early in the morning of July 5th.

In all, he was hospitalised for a little over three weeks – but there can have been no point at which anyone dealing with his case seriously believed he had any chance of recovery and, to my mind, he should have been allowed to die well before he did. It is my belief that his life – thus his suffering – was needlessly and cruelly prolonged.

I can make no complaints about the nursing staff. About the doctors and surgeons I am far less sure. It seems to me that some doctors and surgeons dealing with patients suffering from Aids-related illness clearly have great difficulty confronting their own inability to succeed. Thus – certainly in Ian's case – they prolonged treatment way beyond the point at which it would serve any useful purpose and, more to the point, way, way beyond the point at which it was ethically correct.

On my penultimate visit to Ian (on June 29th, whilst he was still in Intensive Therapy), he was fading from life and dignity; on my final visit (on July 4th, when he'd been returned to Thomas Macaulay Ward) he was bone loosely held together by flesh, bleeding from every orifice, quite devoid of any dignity and no longer Ian. He was an anguished shadow waiting for death. I felt – and will continue to feel until my dying day – that he had been a victim of his doctor's inability to face failure and that the surgery he had undergone (ostensibly to ease his breathing) had been a last ditch experiment on a patient whose symptoms (we had been told) were unique in an effort to discover a little more. Careers are being built on Aids.

Ethically doctors are bound by their oath to heal; ethically too, however, they should know when to stop trying and when to allow their patient release. So far as I am concerned, Ian was kept alive in the interests of Aids research rather than out of any humanitarian concern.

Now because most of us are at least shy of persons in authority, doctors and surgeons can easily intimidate. Because so many people closely involved with Aids patients are neither blood

144

*relatives nor legally empowered to act for them, we have no
rights when it comes to treatment. It seems to me essential that
anyone confronting Aids-related illness (or any other serious
illness) should appoint the person closest to them as next-of-kin
and tell them exactly what they want to happen when they reach
the point at which treatment is clearly proving ineffective.*

*If we can take control in those trying times of the destiny of
our loved ones, much needless suffering can be prevented.*

That at least one of the doctors treating Ian didn't know
when to stop was proved *after* Ian's death – when Lisa,
Alan and I were collecting the documents which we
needed before registering the death.

I had spent no more than a few minutes with Ian on the
day of my final visit. Suddenly nurses and a young
Australian doctor had bustled into the room and –
completely ignoring me – started to do things to Ian.
Perhaps I shouldn't have been there, certainly someone
should have asked me to leave. But no sensitivity was
shown. I slipped quietly from the room and – horror struck
at what had been done to Ian – left the hospital.

Now the young Australian doctor who had so infuriated
me the day before came into the room where Alan and Lisa
and I were waiting for the documents which would enable
us to register his death. "I imagine you can guess what I'm
going to ask," he said. "We would like to go on using Ian's
body in the interest of medical science."

Maybe we were wrong, but we refused permission –
feeling that the interests of medical science had been well
enough served as Ian edged towards death.

✳ ✳ ✳ ✳ ✳

Not enough people know that funerals can be arranged to
their own design. Because it is the convention to have an
officiating priest, mumbled prayers, half remembered
hymns and a usually inappropriate text from the bible,
doesn't mean that that's the way it has to be. A self-
arranged service which is entirely appropriate to the life
and death of the person who has died becomes a far more

satisfying expression of communal grief than a service that neither has meaning for the quick or the dead.

Alan, Lisa and I agreed that Ian should have the appropriate funeral – if it doesn't sound too odd, one that he would have enjoyed. Thus the service opened with John Lennon singing 'Imagine' (in these circumstances a real tear jerker) and closed with the Marvelettes singing 'When You're Young and in Love' (more tears but also uplifting). Between the two songs, Tom Wakefield read an address I'd written about Ian – in which I very carefully included points of reference for all the people attending (friends, lovers, relations, colleagues from work, union comrades).

The service was structured in such a way that all present were able to express their grief *publicly* and – thus – feel that important sense of relief that fully expressed grief brings. It seems to me vitally important to allow emotions to manifest themselves – as otherwise unresolved grief will leave a residue that is hard to expunge.

Without wishing to appear obsessively Victorian about death, I would like to stress my conviction that the rituals of mourning are an all-important part of the healing process. Not that I believe in the traditional and denominational impedimenta of mourning. It is rather my view that each of us has to define the method and duration of our mourning.

For example, on the night of his death, two of us sat *shivah* for Ian. Now I don't possess any formal religious beliefs – but I don't mind borrowing from various expressions of faith whatever suits my purpose. Shivah (from the Hebrew 'seven') is a Jewish ritual when, for seven days, mourners grieve for the deceased. We adapted. From 4am until 11am (when I left for London), we sat with candles burning, entirely fitting Tamla Motown playing, drinking wine and talking about Ian. This was all highly emotional – but also healthy purging of the first out-pourings of our distress.

At the funeral, just before the second song, we hijacked a Quaker expression of feeling – when all those present embraced those nearest to them. Physical comforting is

146

important.

On the day after the funeral and according to his wishes, we scattered Ian's ashes from a windswept hilltop Buddhist shrine in Hertfordshire. Two weeks after that simple ceremony, I held a 'last' party – lots of food, lots of drink, lots of Motown and lots of conversation. Of course, Ian was the core of the party – even though he was not physically present, but because we were able to come together in an essentially cheerful setting and talk about him, this represented another step towards easing of loss.

The final act of 'official mourning' will have taken place between my writing this and its appearance in print. We will be planting a commemorative bed of roses in my garden. A reminder of course – but also a final act which, three months after his death, will allow each of us to acknowledge that we have fittingly mourned Ian and that now (as he was so fond of saying) "Life goes on."

✻ ✻ ✻ ✻ ✻

We didn't condescend. We didn't pretend. Ian was no fool and I am quite certain he knew he was going to die.

"I won't be coming out of here," he managed to say to me one afternoon just before he finally lost all powers of communication. "How long have we known each other?"

It was his fortieth birthday.

"Twenty three years," I answered. "It's a very long time."

He squeezed my hand.

Though we all know it is inevitable, death sometimes seems very final. Yet we must always remember that those we have loved never really die – for they have so enriched our lives they become part of us and remain with us for ever. Whilst there is memory, we remember.

GAY TIMES November 1988

THE PROSPECT OF ROTTERDAM

`Rotterdam is the largest port in the world,' declare Martin Dunford and Jack Holland in their useful *The Rough Guide to Amsterdam and Holland*. 'As you approach the waterfront huge cranes rise up on the horizon, the machinery for handling 300 million tonnes of fuel, grain and materials needed or sold by western Europe each year.

`Totally destroyed by wartime bombing,the city's docks and centre were quickly and imaginatively built, its Lijnebaan the first of Europe's pedestrian shopping precincts. This prospect of docks and shops probably sounds unalluring, but Rotterdam is a surprisingly likeable place . . . '

Even that final qualifying clause in Dunford and Holland's introductory passage to their chapter on 'the largest port in the world' hardly encourages the tourist to think of Rotterdam as a prospective destination. And, it seemed at the time, a more improbable spot could not have been chosen for the second annual meeting of the Association of Lesbian and Gay Writers in Europe (ALGWE) which was the focal point of a week long festival celebrating gay literature and the arts (split between the de Doelen concert hall and congress centre – rather akin to London's Festival Hall – and the Rotterdamse Schouwburg – the city's equivalent to London's Barbican or National Theatre).

That the whole event was to involve gay men and women from all over Europe (including from Iron Curtain countries) *and* interested members of the Rotterdam general public caused images of mobs shivering in icy winds off the North Sea whilst trapped in a relatively bleak semi-industrial landscape.

As it turned out, the reality couldn't have been more different.

✻✻✻✻✻

`The festival was beautifully organised and demonstrated an enlightenment on the part of the Dutch arts sponsorship that would have la Kellet-Bowman and Geoffrey Dickens in the feline labour ward for weeks,' commented novelist Patrick Gale. 'For all the inevitable whinging about non-representation of a minorities' minorities, it was rather like going to an exclusively gay university. Useful contacts for gay publishing and translation were being made in a way that could never happen at the Frankfurt Book Fair, and there was a lot of genuine cross-fertilisation of opinion and ideas. I came home light-headed from the cultural bombardment, buoyed-up by the sense of warm support from Over There and also faintly disturbed at the realisation that British gay men and women are now considered an oppressed group – officially.'

Tom Wakefield, another of the sizeable contingent (which also included Paul Binding, Michael *Sucking Sherbet Lemons* Carson, Maureen Duffy and David Rees), was equally impressed. 'Only a fool could fail to enjoy such an event,' he remarked. 'And only the Dutch could extend such wonderful courtesy and organisational skills to so many different women and men from countries all over Europe. An extraordinary experience . . . '

Perhaps a gay literary festival and conference may seem of rather limited interest – but it's worth bearing in mind that we are what we read and that (to a certain degree) the discussion and exchanges of ideas which took place during that hectic week (`genuine cross-fertilisation') will bear fruit in the novels, works of non-fiction and journalism that gay men and women will be writing in the future and which will percolate around Europe (for starters) in the months and years to come.

Patrick Gale's observation that 'British gay men and women are now considered an oppressed group – officially' demands consideration – not least because it represents an opinion that any British gay man or lesbian travelling in mainland Europe is likely to encounter if they enter into discussion with local gay men or women in any given European country. For however much the British may be accused of being insular, it must be recognised that mainland Europeans are no more familiar with the structure and workings of our society (and the sub-structure which particularly concerns us) than we are with theirs.

During our five days in Rotterdam (we were a group of three connected – primarily – with the festival's theatre programme) we had many conversations (on the festival sites and in various of the pleasant bars we frequented after festival hours) which clearly indicated to us that gay men and lesbians within continental Europe view their British counterparts (particularly because of Section 28) as living under a fascistic regime which almost totally disallows freedom of expression – most especially freedom of sexual expression.

`The Iron Lady wants to ban homosexuality from public life in England,' said Peter, a Dutch marine we chatted to over glasses of freshly-squeezed orange juice (available in all the bars). 'Here we have liberty of speech, liberty of work and liberty of sex,' he continued. 'To do what Margaret Thatcher wants to do would cause a riot here.' Our conversation with Peter rambled around the subject of repression in England (people rarely speak of 'Britain') but the brief lines quoted succinctly encapsulate the view of Britain held by many of the people to whom we spoke.

The suggestion that Margaret Thatcher and her government are jack-booted Nazi-clones denying gay men and women any means of expression made us – if not nationalistic – defensive. After all, a great deal of what can be described as gay culture (much of it successfully exported around the world) comes out of the British Isles – and if there were statistical charts available they would almost certainly prove that there is more going on in this country of particular (though not exclusive) interest to gay men and women than there is in any other country in Europe.

Consider this list of home-grown products: Hugh Whitemore's *Breaking the Code* (recently staged at the Rotterdamse Schwouburg, incidentally), Julian Mitchell's *Another Country*, Michael Wilcox's *Rents* (regularly in production around the country); *Maurice*, *The Fruit Machine*,

My Beautiful Laundrette, any film by Derek Jarman; Boy George, Erasure, The Communards, David Hockney, Gilbert and George, Francis Bacon; *The Swimming Pool Library, Hiroshima Joe, The Aerodynamics of Pork* . . . And that's without considering the output of companies like Gay Sweatshop or Gay Men's Press.

And is there any other country in Europe which has so large and varied a gay press as that which now exists in this country? We have *Gay Times, HIM, Capital Gay, The Pink Paper, Square Peg* and the *European Gay Review* – not to mention more localised publications such as *Gay Scotland.* Not bad for a small country cowering under a repressive government which doesn't allow expression of sexuality.

If only there were funding or sponsorship for a truly representative festival of British gay culture along the lines of Rotterdam's Satisfaction Festival. But that's a real pipe dream.

* * * * *

But what of the city itself?

Rotterdam is a small provincial city and most of the places we either needed or wanted to get to were within easy walking distance of our hotels; however, if we hadn't felt inclined to walk there seemed an ample number of big yellow trams to transport us about. A walk to the waterfront led along to a fun-fair and park – and then we thought we'd lost ourselves. As almost everyone appeared to speak some English, we found ourselves without difficulty directed to the appropriate tram back to the city centre.

In some respects Rotterdam very much resembles any provincial British city of a similar size – although it is much cleaner and almost entirely lacking in the hostile atmosphere always so much in evidence in our own urban and metropolitan communities. Although Rotterdam city centre could be almost anywhere in the world that has succumbed to the horrors of precincts and malls – the Doelen is about as architecturally exciting as the Festival

151

Hall – the outer limits had a certain charm, much enhanced because of abundant green parks and the presence of water.

`Rotterdam is a city of workmen,' Koos de Wilt, one of the festival organisers had told us as he escorted us to the Schwouburg theatre complex, 'and they do not much go to the theatre.' Certainly the facilities exist – the Schwouburg, for instance, has a main house (a multi-media piece with music by Philip Glass was receiving its premiere whilst we were there) and a two hundred seater studio (in which the festival's theatre events took place).

Our brief experience of Rotterdam certainly didn't leave us feeling we were in a cultural void – there seemed to be a range on theatres, cinemas and museums and galleries.

`Amsterdam has more by way of gay life,' Peter – the marine – told us a trifle apologetically. 'In Rotterdam you have to search for it a bit.'

Fortunately those of us attending the festival had been provided with information packs which included a listing of gay venues. We only visited bars – though these were very different from the kind of bars we were used to at home. Food was served in most, the atmosphere was welcoming and the clientele friendly – or maybe we just looked like the little lost tourists. The Mateloos (Nieuwe Binnenweg 105) was the first we discovered – fortuitously, as it turned out, for many of the other venues on the list we had been given were in the same neighbourhood (De Zwarte Kat, Cafe Proost, Literair cafe de Overheid and Bonaparte amongst them). No small list, that, for a provincial town – and there were many more bars and cafes and a discotheque on the list.

*****

Rotterdam hadn't sounded the most promising of destinations and – ultimately – we couldn't claim to have explored it in any depth. What we did discover – however – was that the largest port in the world has more than 300 million tonnes of fuel, grain and materials . . . We had to leave Rotterdam mid-way through the festival, we did so with regret and agreed that it was a city we'd be happy to return to.

GAY TIMES February 1989

SAPPHO AT THE STOVE

`This is by way of an excuse and an explanation. I have written this book more or less in self-defence, because I am tired of people eyeing me, and then remarking: "You know you don't *look* as if you could cook – I am surprised,"' Naomi Jacob (known to her friends as 'Mickie') wrote at the beginning of *Me – In the Kitchen* (1935). 'I may add that they are usually the same type of person who says: "Fancy you having a Peke – I should have thought that a Great Dane or a really sporting Fox Terrier would have been so much more your line of country."'

`Mickie' Jacob – a prolific and popular novelist best remembered for a long sequence of novels about a Jewish family (`The Gollancz Saga' – *Founder of the House*, *That Wild Lie*, *Young Emmanuel*, *Four Generations*, *Private Gollancz* and several others easily enough unearthed in secondhand bookshops, usually in the Book Club editions) – always dressed in a style best described as 'mannish' (slacks and shirts) and because of this those people who eyed her made that ridiculous assumption that because she looked and probably behaved in a 'masculine' manner she was incapable of 'feminine' pursuits. 'These people, it is hardly necessary for me to add, generally know as much about cookery as they do about Pekes . . . The fact remains that I can cook, and that I do keep a Peke.'

The basic misconception that the ill-informed *still* make about gay men – that they are ersatz women and thus must be able to perform 'womanly' duties such as cooking – is turned around when it comes to lesbians; because the ill-informed consider lesbians ersatz men, it follows that they must be incapable of performing 'womanly' tasks like cooking – though these same people might possibly imagine that they might be handy with a hammer and nails.

To my certain knowledge, there is no lesbian counterpart to Rick Leed's *Dinner for Two* (a self-styled cook book for gay men). But one of the most famous of all books about food was compiled by a lesbian: *The Alice B Toklas Cook*

155

Book (1954, available in an elegant new edition from Brilliance Books).

Alice B Toklas, lover and shadow of the American writer-in-exile-in-Paris Gertrude Stein (the stone on their joint grave – shaped like a double bed – in the Père Lachaise in Paris has Gertrude on the front and Alice tucked away at the back), compiled her book 'during the first three months of an attack of pernicious jaundice'. It was written 'as an escape from the narrow diet and monotony of illness, and I daresay nostalgia for old days and old ways and remembered health and enjoyment lent special lustre to dishes and menus barred from an invalid table, but hovering dream-like in invalid memory'.

The Alice B Toklas Cook Book achieved a kind of notoriety because it contained a recipe for hash cookies (though my 1960 American reprint doesn't include this). Alice B – who provided Stein with her most readable and popular book (*The Autobiography of Alice B Toklas*) – mixes reminiscences and recipes to provide a book of immense charm and a less certain practicality.

Colette defies any kind of conventional sexual label – she had relationships with women and men but is most accurately described as a sensual being because her pleasure in sensation absorbed every aspect of her living and her passion for 'Missy' (her lover, the Marquise de Belheuf) or Maurice Goudeket (her third husband) or her animals, plants or food are all recorded with a high level of exultation. Madame Colette writes beautifully about food – the following from *Break of Day*, for example:

> In honour of a local saint, who according to tradition presides over merry-making Segonzac, Carco, Regis, Gignoux and Therese Dorny were to leave their hillside and eat a southern luncheon here: salads, stuffed racasse* and aubergine fritters, an everyday meal which I usually enliven with a roast bird . . . "Vial, don't you think they'll like my sauce with the little chickens? Four little chickens split in half,

beaten with the flat of the chopper, salted, peppered, and anointed with pure oil brushed on with a sprig pebreda?** The little leaves of pebreda, and the taste of it, cling to the grilled flesh. Look at them, don't they look good?"

Though Colette never produced a cook book, food is so much a component of her writing that she fits neatly into this survey. The extract from *Break of Day* functions well as a recipe – ingredients and instructions are both in that brief passage of dialogue. Incidentally, the 'four little chickens' – sometimes referred to as 'spring chickens' – was clearly a favourite of Colette's: variations of this recipe crop up in other of her books – including the sublime *Cheri/The Last of Cheri* which positively bursts with loving descriptions of food.

In her recently published (auto)`biographical' novel *Jigsaw* the novelist Sybille Bedford writes extensively about food and food preparation. Towards the end of an opening passage describing her earliest memories, Mrs Bedford writes of: 'The infants' table-d'hote at the hotel. There is a lot of window and it is very light. In front of each plate, in front of my plate, there stands a small china bowl. In it there is cream and in the cream – delight – there floats a whole round yolk of egg, uncooked egg. The egg in cream is to be put into our food. Nannies sit behind us in a circle ready to interfere. I am entirely determined to handle my own egg, to choose whether to stir it into my soup, my spinach or my mashed potatoes and I win.' This early recollection – Mrs Bedford suggests – is an indication of a trend to come: a 'great love of cookery'. Certainly throughout this particular book food and food preparation are used to 'place' the various characters who move through Mrs Bedford's fictionalised (?) life.

In the years between the two world wars, the name of

---

* The mediterranean fish many people consider an essential ingredient of bouillabaisse.
** *Thymus pulegiodes* – proven_al thyme, sometimes known as donkey thyme.

Constance Spry was synonymous with that most 'feminine' of occupations, flower arrangement. Spry's cleverly constructed displays of flowers were a feature of society homes and functions and she was pre-eminent in the field. It was – therefore – particularly fascinating to discover from Diana Souhami's brilliantly contrived biography of the painter Gluck that she and Spry were lovers. In post-war years, when the demand for flower arrangement had diminished, Spry turned her talents in other directions – the monumental *The Constance Spry Cookery Book* (Co-written with Rosemary Hume). Running to over twelve hundred pages, this is the kind of food compendium that many 1950's brides must have found amongst their wedding presents.

Nancy Spain, who along with her lover Joan Werner Laurie was killed in a 'plane crash in 1964, was a great-niece of Isabella Beeton, most well-known of the Victorian writers on food and household management. Spain (who usually dressed in casual slacks and open necked shirts) was a journalist of note and a popular television performer – sometimes performing an amusing (for insiders) double act with the gay Gilbert Harding on programmes like *Juke Box Jury*. Besides penning a biography study of her famous ancestor – *Mrs Beeton and Her Husband* – Nancy Spain also put together *The Nancy Spain Colour Cook Book* (the frontispiece is a portrait of the author with frying pan). Though certain of Ms Spain's books are easily enough found (particularly the posthumously published *A Funny Thing Happened On The Way*), the cook book has become something or a rarity, so much so that one specialist in the field didn't even know of its existence.

Perhaps the closest lesbian approximation to Rick Leed's *Dinner For Two* is *Turning The Tables: Recipes and Reflections From Women*. 'This book would raise some of the many issues and political points which food raises for us as feminists and radicals, issues which pose themselves in different ways for Black women and white women, feminists, working class and middle class women in "affluent" countries, women in "third world" countries, lesbians and heterosexual women, mothers, daughters, etc, etc,' Sue O'Sullivan, compiler of the collection, explains in her Introduction. But though the book includes recipes and reflections from the likes of The Chinese Lesbian Group, Jill Posener and Miriam Margoyles, it cannot be honestly described as a cookbook for lesbians.

Of course there can never really be such a thing as a lesbian or gay cookbook; what on earth would come under the classification of lesbian or gay food? What we eat is dictated by taste diet and economics rather than sexual preference . . .

A listing in a book catalogue for *The Book of Etiquette* by Lady Troubridge set my pulse racing; Had Una Troubridge, consort of Radclyffe Hall (who must stand in relation to lesbian history in much the same position as does Oscar Wilde in gay male history), put together a two volume book on how to behave and how to treat the servants? It seemed all too likely.

Alas, *The Book of Etiquette* turned out to have been written by *Laura* Troubridge, clearly related in marriage to the more famous Una. There was a connection – but tenuous at best. And what of Radclyffe Hall and Una Troubridge? How did they cope in the kitchen? They had servants . . .

GAY TIMES June 1989

PLAYING UP ...

`The Boys in the Band has been running in London for a year,' I wrote in 1969 in an article which looked at recent gay plays (`Whoops! A sad gay racket', *Jeremy*, Volume 1, Number 5), 'for even longer in New York, where we are shortly to be treated to a film version of it. The play has had the dubious distinction of being issued on a set of long-playing records ... But *The Boys in the Band* shows the unpleasant, outrageous picture of homosexuality that is good for press and public alike, Why? Because the homosexuals are of the lisping, mincing, perfume-reeking, mother-ridden kind. *Boys* is ... most offensive in this respect and is a pretty poorly written play on top of that. Isn't it basically two one-act plays, one comedy and one drama, tied together to make a full-length piece?'

❋ ❋ ❋ ❋ ❋

I'd hated the play. I remember sitting through the first preview at Wyndham's theatre with an increasing sense of rage. To me, the play was incredibly offensive. But that first London audience (a particularly *homosexual* audience) rose to its collective feet at the end of the evening and cheered. "It's a night of triumph for *us*," someone nearby commented. "I didn't think *we'd* ever be so honestly portrayed on stage ... "

Yet this was the play (the film followed in 1970) which included such lines as 'You show me a happy homosexual, and I'll show you a gay corpse' and 'if we ... if we could just ... not hate ourselves so much. That's it, you know. If we could just *learn* not to hate ourselves quite so very much.'

Though involved with the beginnings of the British gay press (froth rather than politics), I wouldn't have described myself as politicized. I'm sure I didn't use expressions like 'self-repressive' or 'self-loathing' – but, essentially, that's how I viewed the play. Had the expression been in circulation, I think I'd have described *The Boys in the Band* as 'homophobic'.

the play – which sprang out of Crowley's analysis (paid for by his friend Natalie Wood) – has had a bumpy rite of passage: politically suspect (at very least), it has been reviled for years. But . . . Twenty one years on, what does one make of it?

The Boys in the Band was pre-Stonewall, pre Gay Liberation, pre-the libertinism of the Seventies and very much pre-Aids. It was also something of a one-off – a kind of unique lumbering dinosaur, Broadway's first commercially successful play about homosexuals and – it is worth noting – the last until Harvey Fierstien's *Torch Song Trilogy* (`The most truly conservative play to come along in years . . . ' Jack Kroll, *Newsweek*) reached the Little Theatre in 1982 (four years after the first of the trilogy had been staged at La Mama). Crowley's play was also a kind of full-stop. After *Boys in the Band*, there wouldn't again be a play about homosexuality in which homosexuals were so tortured *by their homosexuality*.

The Boys in the Band is a post- *Who's Afraid of Virginia Woolf?* confrontational lay. But, unlike Edward Albee's masterpiece, Crowley's opus has no resolution. By the end of *Virginia Woolf*, we know we have witnessed a painful expression of love and need. By the end of *Boys*, we realise that we – like the nine men on stage – have been set up. In truth *Boys* is a disaster movie in which nine people are thrown together for no better reason than they'll react to each other. Outside the confines of the play and movie, there's little reason to believe that any of the characters would know each other.

Set in the apartment of free-loader Michael (witty but sharp-tongued), *Boys* gathers together a mix`n'match collection of faggots who are to celebrate the birthday of Harold (`a thirty-two-year-old, ugly, pock-marked jew fairy'). Amongst the guests are Emory (`Connie casserole', an outrageous queen who is so effeminate that he's in a permanent state of gender confusion), Bernard (black and humpy but who has always been in love with the white son of the house where his mother cleans) and promiscuous Larry (his theme song could be 'so many men, so little time') and his in-the-process of getting a divorce lover Hank. Crowley believes in dishing out the stereotypes with a vengeance.

During the course of the party – interrupted by a straight friend of Michael's – the characters bitch and snarl, provoke tears and draw blood (actually and metaphorically). The first act (or first half of the film) is waspishly funny, the second half is real torture. Like Albee's George and Martha, Crowley's partygoers have their own version of 'Get the guests' – a tiresome Truth or Dare game played on the telephone.

During the course of the play/movie ('The action is continuous and occurs one evening within the time necessary to perform the script.') there is much camp, more bitchery and an attempt to find some eternal truths about the homosexual condition. None of them very pleasant.

It was only recently, after reviewing *The Boys in the Band* on video, that I perceived a subtle sub-text – which may have more to do with my interpretation than with Crowley's writing. Though Harold (a wonderfully sinister portrayal by the late Leonard Frey) and Emory are faggots of the stereotypical breed so beloved by the general public and the tabloid press, they are fighters and survivors. Harold combats hostility with a sharp tongue and a degree of self-awareness; Emory fights back with sheer flamboyance. Cowboy (the hunky hustler Emory has 'bought' as Harold's birthday present) might be a bimbo – but (unlike Joe Orton's Mr Sloane, for example) he's really rather lovable.

The most positive aspects – as Vito Russo has pointed out in *The Celluloid Closet: Homosexuality in the Movies* (Harper & Rowe, 1981) – are presented via Larry and Hank: 'who are both just as "queer" as Emory yet look as straight as Alan. The possibility that there could be non-stereotypical homosexuals who are also staunch advocates of a working gay relationship is presented by the lovers throughout the film. And these are the two characters most

163

often ignored by critics and analysts of the film. It is Larry who speaks of rejecting heterosexual concepts of marriage and creating a relationship with "respect for one another's freedom, with no need to lie or pretend."' It has to be acknowledged, however, that Larry and Hank's relationship is very evidently doomed to disaster because though fine words are spoken about living without lies, Hank will never come to terms with nor accept Larry's particular freedoms.

Ultimately *The Boys in the Band* has to be viewed as a period piece – it certainly couldn't be re-staged today as anything other than an historical drama. It remains – of course – hatefully entertaining. But for all its success all those years ago, *Boys* didn't do a great deal for any of the participants. Except for one further (*un*successful) play, Crowley hasn't been heard of since; Robert La Tourneaux (`Cowboy') ended his career as a male stripper in New York and is now dead; Leonard Frey appeared in movies like *Fiddler on the Roof* and *Jesus Christ Superstar*, but was never again given a role as meaty as that of Harold; Kenneth Nelson (Michael) has been more regularly seen on British stages than in Hollywood movies. And so it goes . .

GAY TIMES March 1990

THE WAY WE WORE

Britain in the Nineteen-Fifties was living in a state of austerity. Though the victors, reconstruction after a crippling world war was slow. What was heralded as a New Elizabethan Age when Queen Elizabeth II came to the throne in 1952 was about as invigorating as a spam fritter.

Britain was uniformly drab – nowhere more so than in the limited range of clothing available to young men. In his *Costumes and Fashion*, James Laver doesn't even refer to male fashion in his chapter on the dawning 'era of individualism'. In the literature of fashion, it is the following decade which hogs the most attention. But the roots of the 'Swingin' Sixties' style were firmly planted in the Fifties.

To get any impression of what passed for style in the late Fifties (for example), it is necessary to go back to novels such as Terry Taylor's *Baron's Court, All Change* (1961); Colin Spencer's *Anarchists in Love* (1963); or Colin MacInnes's *Absolute Beginners* (1959). Memoirs of the period are occasionally some help. *Stamp Album* and *Coming Attraction* (the first two of Terence Stamp's three volume autobiography) are particularly useful as the actor-as-young-man was especially clothes conscious.

✳ ✳ ✳ ✳ ✳

Michael: The jean was essentially an item of work clothing; it didn't become a fashion item for some years.

Peter: When I was about thirteen (1958), friends at school who wore jeans wore them because their parents couldn't afford proper trousers. Ironically, though my parents couldn't afford to dress me well, I craved a pair of jeans. Probably because the boys at school whom I fancied wore them. So even at that stage, certain items of clothing inspired a (subconscious) sexual charge. It was an up-hill battle to convince my mother and father to buy me a pair of jeans and a pair of sneakers (people wore sneakers because they couldn't afford proper shoes) because – though we were Eastenders – they thought both common.

Michael: Most clothes for men were drab and dreary. My influences when I was growing up in Luton were from American magazines like *Esquire* – which I don't remember having fashion spreads as we know them now, but did have advertisements for clothes which were all stylised up and looked very glamorous. It was a dream world. The clothes weren't available in the shops and I never saw people wearing clothes like that – I suppose because there was nowhere near as much tourism and the clothes I was seeing in *Esquire* were *American* clothes. I suppose the only place we saw men wearing stylish leisure wear was in Hollywood movies.

Peter: Certainly hairstyles were influenced by American performers.

Michael: The 'Tony Curtis' was probably the most famous . . .

Peter: I remember mine was cut short and smooth in a 'Perry Como' . . .

Michael: Most men had their hair cut in a traditional short back 'n' sides, which of course is fashionable today.

Peter: Very evidently, the 'Tony Curtis' and the 'Perry Como' were the forerunners of hairstyles worn by the two predominant youth groups of the next decade: The Mods and the Rockers.

Michael: Cecil Gee – notable the big store that used to be in Shaftesbury Avenue – carried what could be described as an American Casual range. It was very glamorous and very expensive. It was an Ivy League look. I bought my first pair of chinos from Cecil Gee. They were high-waisted, tight-fitting cotton trousers without pleats that were based upon American army fatigues (military casual wear) gussied up via a gay sensibility.

Peter: America wasn't the only influence, though. There was a distinctly Italian look in the late Fifties. When I was about fourteen, I was kitted-out in an Italian style 'bum-freezer' jacket, fairly tapered trousers and pointy-toe shoes made from woven leather. It was a very neat – on me, because I'm small, petite – look.

Michael: The Italian look emphasised the figure. The jackets were short – that's why they were called 'bum-freezers' – and the trousers tight to emphasise the bum and the crotch.

Peter: I've always considered that the beginnings of re-eroticising of the male

Michael: At the same time, shirts became softer. What we now know as polo shirts – knitted wool shirts which slip on over the head, usually with three buttons and a soft collar – came into fashion. They were definitely Italian-influenced. At the same time, too, colours became softer. Younger men – and clearly younger *gay* men – obviously didn't feel it so necessary to project such aggressively 'masculine' images.

Peter: For the first time in decades, it was almost acceptable for young men to look sexy.

Michael: 'Vince' – whoever he was – was the great designer for gay men in that period. His catalogues were snapped up as if they were gay pin-up magazines. He started off in a little slip road off Carnaby Street and eventually ended up in Carnaby Street. I think Vince started Carnaby Street rather than John Stephen – though John Stephen refined the Vince look and made it street acceptable. Vince clothes were very close-cut and figure-hugging. They showed the shape and were totally unlike anything in British high street fashion which remained rigidly conservative. For anyone who could get to London and Vince, the clothes were a real identity statement.

Peter: That's a point that's worth emphasising: stylish clothes for young gay men in those days had a lot to do with where you were. And, perhaps, something to do with which class you came from. A great deal of the style was rooted in London working-class gay men working their way out from under.

GAY TIMES May 1990

SWEET DREAMS

After being queer-bashed (and writing about it) I received several letters from men who had been through the same experience. One such letter has remained in my memory – simply because the writer suggested a kind of Mosaic retribution (an eye for an eye, a tooth for a tooth) against any queer-bashers who were ever apprehended.

In effect, what the writer was proposing was that we (the victims) be allowed to punish the perpetrators by inflicting on them injuries identical to those that they caused us. Thus, had those who'd done me over ever been caught, I'd have been empowered to break a few arms, crack a few wrists and give a severe kicking to several sets of kidneys.

At the time, I was quite appalled. Never a violent person, I believed then (and – I have to confess – believe now) that violence breeds violence and that such retribution would provoke more of what it was trying to prevent. However . . .

However, as the years have passed on by and the tide of violence against gay men and lesbians continues to rise, I've found myself more-and-more indulging in sweet dreams of revenge . . .

My local pub – within spitting distance of the house – is a haunt of violent yobs. These people – men *and* women – inhabit a twilight world of verbal and physical aggression (the word 'fuck' is a kind of punctuation) and on one memorable occasion they subjected the entire street to a small-scale riot during the course of which they smashed every window in the pub, attempted to batter down the doors with scaffolding ripped from an adjacent building and wrecked five parked cars.

At various times, these people have shouted anti-gay or Aids abuse at the house. Once a projectile was lobbed through my bedroom window. Curiously, I've found the verbal attacks more alarming than that specific instance of physical violence – thereby proving the old adage about sticks and stone quite wrong. Words do hurt . . .

169

On the opening night of one of the town's most successful gay venues – well before they'd got a door policy together – I was called a fat queer by a gang of straight thugs who were hanging out in the toilets (presumably with the singular intention of abusing the gay men for whom the particular night had been established).

Horrified, frightened and rather ashamed (the latter at my own cowardice for not responding), I scuttled back to the friends with whom I'd been drinking and insisted that we leave. I did eventually receive an apology from a member of the club's management – and a door policy was subsequently implemented. But many's the time I've brooded about this (and similar) incidents and wished I'd had both the bottle and the brawn to front-up such people and maybe give *them* a good thumping.

As the straight world continues its hostilities – and I'm increasingly of the view that we don't have *any* friends out there *whatever their class* – I frequently find myself wishing I wasn't so nelly, merely wallowing in fantasies of revenge in which, for example, I firebomb the local pub when it's at its bigoted busiest, or thump someone who's called me a poof.

*****

Terry Sanderson's recent Press Council victory over *The Sun*'s Gary Bushell was satisfying – but, as subsequent issues of that publication have shown, not terribly effective. 'We must defeat militant gay cult' trumpeted Bushell in a 'personal view' piece a few days after the ruling. Mr Bushell's rabid ravings seemed – if anything – more intense. How pleasant, however, those fantasies of ripping off his head and shoving it where the monkey stuffed nuts . . .

That's why I found director Peter Medak and writer Philip Ridley's film *The Krays* so uplifting.

'I didn't feel any shame then – and I don't feel any now,' Ron Kray has written. 'It was the way I was born. There is

170

nothing necessarily weak about a homosexual man – and I believe he does no wrong provided he does not force his attentions on anyone who doesn't want them. I hate people who pick on homosexuals. I hate words like 'queer' and 'poof' ... A gangster called me 'a fat poof' – and died for it.'

Ridley's screenplay doesn't glamorise violence and it doesn't glamorise the Krays. In particular, Ron Kray is shown as a highly manipulative psychopath – and the thought of becoming an object of his desire must have made many a young man's blood run cold. But, probably because he himself is gay, Ridley doesn't fudge the issue of Ron Kray's homosexuality: it is presented as a statement of fact, acknowledged, whether they like it or loath it, by all the essential characters in the film. Ron Kray's sexual preferences are certainly not seen as a weakness (it's worth remembering that he was always known as 'The Colonel') and it might possibly be read as a strength.

✳ ✳ ✳ ✳ ✳

Not that I'm exactly advocating taking Ron Kray as either a hero or a rôle-model. Yet I did find something very positive about the image of this particular gay man fighting a particular irrational prejudice in the only way he knew how: with violence. For me, there was something really vital about the sequence of the film in which Gary Kemp as Ron Kray sets out to blow the brains out of George Cornell because he's called him 'a fat poof' once too often.

Written by Ridley and played by Steven Berkoff as a raving Bushell-type homophobe, Cornell is every queen's nightmare. Most of us have been subjected to some kind of anti-gay abuse at some time in our lives – even if it is *only* via a television screen or a newspaper (and the more intellectual 'papers – whatever their liberal credentials – are no more fond of us than the tabloids). So I don't imagine I'm on my own when I admit that I was inwardly cheering as the gun went off – and Cornell slumped to the floor.

This was a sweet dream of revenge fulfilled. I felt a positive sense of elation – and perhaps a little stronger. As I bowled out of the cinema, just for a minute, I almost believed I'd thump the first person to call me a queer . . .

GAY TIMES July 1990

SUBVERSIVES!

Way back in the 1950s, when radio and television announcers spoke BBC English and the uses of literacy were perhaps taken more seriously, American comic books (many, like American B-movies, a reflection of Cold War paranoia) were damned and banned in Britain for fear of the pernicious influence they might exert on the sceptred isle's impressionable youth.

This was a manoeuvre that didn't quite work – because hard on the heels of comic book heroes were flesh 'n' blood heroes like Marlon Brando and James Dean and Elvis Presley who were destined (doomed?) to have far more enduring effects than anything coming off newsprint pages.

The comic book faded into obscurity, the *almost* exclusive preserve of kid brothers and sisters who believed in Batman, Superman and Captain America for just about as long as Santa Claus had credibility. They were essentially *juvenile*. As a force with anything to say and possessing any kind of influence, the comic book seemed dead.

However, in the Eighties comics (or comix) came back with a vengeance. But these comics were different. The form had been re-invented.

The writers and artists who produced them were no longer intent on presenting superheroes in designer longjohns set to save the world – or, rather, America, most commonly a version of New York City – from dictatorial enemies of corporate capitalism. *That* comic book Age of Innocence was past . . .

The new crop of comics (now sometimes somewhat grandly designated 'graphic novels' to give them a needless respectability) focused on a world in distress in which there were no more certainties and in which villains rather than sporting snazzy disguises (`The Joker', 'The Penguin', 'Cat Woman') were all too often faceless bureaucrats working for anonymous extremists (`Resurrection crusade', 'Damnation Army', 'Tongues of Fire') who want a return to 'Victorian values'.

The new breed of comics is street smart. The new breed of comics had *attitude*. To be precise: enemies in the comics of the Fifties symbolised an *irrational* fear of the Left; enemies in comics of the Eighties and Nineties symbolise an all too *rational* fear of the New Right.

For example, Jamie Delano, John Ridgway and Alfredo Alcala's *John Constantine: Hellblazer* – originally created by Alan Moore, whose *Swamp Thing* was the progenitor of much that was to follow – is set in a recognizable *now*. 'Constantine's world is (demons apart) our own world,' horror novelist Clive Barker has written. 'These are stories that touch upon the issues of the day: Aids, nuclear waste, the rise of neo-Nazism, street violence . . . '

The 1989 *Annual* opens with Constantine watching Margaret Thatcher addressing the nation (the world?) at the time of the Falklands War: she is drawn as clearly rabid; he is drawn as a survivor of the excesses of the Sixties, disturbed and irritated, who ultimately puts his foot through the television screen in protest at a return to a jingoism that should long since have died.

Constantine is half avenging angel, half instrument of Satan. He is blond and blue-eyed – but clearly wrecked. He has evidently drunk deeply from a heady Sixties brew of peace 'n' love 'n' drugs of varying degrees of potency and at least some of the supernatural events which overtake him *could* be the result of drug psychosis. He is ageless but eternal and his adventures encompass hard political attitudes from the agitprop pages of an underground magazine and higher romantics which could have been lifted straight from the pages of *Morte d'Arthur* or *The Song of Roland*.

In part, at least, the new snobbism that is creeping around graphic novels stems from the literacy of the texts – replete with allusions any intellectually alert reader can decode. Similarly, Ridgway and Alcala's graphics range easily between the harshly realistic and a style which has borrowed from everyone between the pre-Raphaelites (who returned to favour in the Sixties) and the likes of H R Giger and Roger Dean (all those fantasy sleeves for endless

Yes albums). Though doubtless read and enjoyed by children (or those these days termed 'young adults'), the new breed of comics are distinctly adult fare.

Nowhere is this change between Fifties comics and the virile new generation more apparent than in attitudes to sexuality.

Superman didn't show so much as a ripple at the fork of his body; Lois Lane might have been occasionally feisty – but she was basically a swooning groupie. Today's adult-orientated comics and graphic novels are suffused with powerful women (see Gilbert Hernandez' *Heartbreak Soup* series or the 'Third World War' serial in *Crisis*), hetero-sexual men and women inter-acting with confusion (see Hernandez, *Crisis*, John Constantine's various exploits), and gay men, particularly, trying to fight repression and prejudice (see, especially, *Hellblazer*, volume two) or as positive heroes (see 'perspectives' in *Crisis*). Today's comics don't pussy-foot around sex – it is present in every complexion, an issue (or set of issues) to be confronted like an other.

Of course, there have been *specifically* gay comics (primarily, but not exclusively American) for some years. A case *could* be argued for the inclusion in this catalogue of the work of Tom of Finland or Quaintance – though as both worked as one-frame narratives, within this context, they might best be considered cartoonists. *Gay Comix* was started in 1980 and the Founding Editor of that series has subsequently gone one to produce *Howard Cruse's Wendel Comix*, which focus on the life of the eponymous hero and his boyfriend Ollie. Britain, too, has produced gay comics, notably *Matt Black: Charcoal*, promoted as the 'first British gay superhero'. Born white to black parents, Matt Black has the ability to carbonise matter – which he uses to combat crime after the murder of his lover. The creation of Don Melia (graphics) and Lionel Gracey-Whitman (text), *Matt Black* allied wit with social concern – but like *Gay Comix* and *Wendel* or David Shenton's *Stanley and the Mask of Mystery* or *Phobia Phobia* is of less concern within this present context because the audience was clearly targeted.

This group of comics *knew* who would be reading them – there can never have been such certainty about the mass-market adult-orientated comics, which is what makes them so wonderfully subversive.

Because comics like *Heartbreak Soup, Deadline* (`Tank Girl'), *Hellblazer, Crisis* or *The Tapping Vein* (adapted from Clive Barker's *Books of Blood*, short stories yet to be surpassed by his elephantine novels) are as likely to be read a National Front supporter, a racist or a homophobe as they are by an appropriately tolerant – for want of a better word – individual, the messages that are implicitly planted in exciting words and pictures are far more likely to have an impact – however slight – than any amount of overt propaganda.

The issues confronted in the comics of the Eighties and Nineties are the issues to which thought must constantly return: racism and sexism, nuclear waste dumping and pollution, homophobia and street violence, religious fundamentalism. Because these subjects are presented in a non-dogmatic form, they are assimilable by the largest number of people. But by no means are the issues cut-and-dried. 'There are three other stories in this volume which, loosely, begin to build a background continuity involving the Resurrection Crusade and the Damnation Army,' Jamie Delano writes in his Introduction to *Hellblazer* (volume two). 'This is basically a tale of everyday hard-line fundamentalist Christians opposed by the devious machinations of hellish fifth-columnists and dirty trick specialists. Who's good – who's evil? Difficult to say – neither side seems to care too much for the well-being of humanity . . . '

Crucial to *John Constantine: Hellblazer*, for example, are four issues (18-21, May-August 1989) which centre around events that begin in the Oscar Wilde hotel in London and focus on a gay investigative journalist for *The Guardian* (shades of Duncan Campbell?) who is under threat from a sinister technocratics company called Geotroniks who are intent upon ultimate power achieved by whatever means they deem acceptable. Eventually abducted by Geotroniks's private police force, the journalist ponders his situation and makes direct reference to something he has read in *Gay Times*.

Naturally the position of lesbians and gay men in early Nineties society isn't the only 'social problem' considered in contemporary comics. But – as a good for-instance – the four episodes of *Hellblazer* briefly outlined above serve as a reminder that fictional use of the plight of a singular gay man in a singular situation *may* provoke at least one homophobe to wonder why he holds the attitudes he does? Why should one group in some way divergent from the prescribed norms of society be made to suffer because of that divergence? Hippies and hippie convoys also figure prominently as a persecuted sub-section of society in these particular comics – which, in some respects, at least, also serve to remind us that society as an entity is made up from a whole mass of social groupings – colonies, as it were, of individuals united by sexuality, religious belief, race, shared ambitions. It is especially interesting to see scientists treated as the new witches – a view that is hardly original (see Walter Miller Jnr's thirty year old science fiction novel *A Canticle for Leibowitz*), but it is a view that will almost certainly gain common currency as scientists are more-and-more seen as the individuals who blight our lives.

Of course, it's easy to intellectualise about contemporary comics – when primarily they are there to entertain. But it is very evident that both the content of comics and graphic novels and the wide sales that they enjoy reflect a general dissatisfaction with the shape of Thatcherite society and that they *may* ultimately cause a change in the thinking of those who read them because they don't want to live at the edge to which the new heroes have tottered – with the rest of us sometimes seeming not that far behind.

With thanks to Howard Luke, for the loan of comics from his collection

GAY TIMES October 1990

177

TEEN IDOLS:
'Are you or have you ever . . . ?'

"Have you ever fancied a member of the same sex?" an anonymous interviewer in the teen magazine *Smash Hits* asked the nubile quartet East 17 (named after the London district from which they hail). "Fancied? In what way? Like, 'Cor, I'd give him one'? Naah. Yeah, I find blokes attractive," admitted Tony (the cute one who seems to be falling out of his clothes in the video for their catchy eco-hit 'House of Love'). "I'm a truthful person, I can admit these things." He also agrees that he'd pose naked for a pornographic magazine "if the money's right. You know, lots of money. A few Os on the end of a one. I'd probably do it for nothing if I was drunk." His admission that he's "not a shy boy" comes as no surprise. The other members of the group – John, Terry and Brian – were far less forthcoming, but in no way evinced the coyness (or even horror) that would have been the usual response a few years back.

"Did you deliberately set out to become gay pin-ups?" Mancunian dollies Take That were asked in an interview in style magazine *The Face*. "No, we never aimed for anything in particular," Gary answered. "We just think that whoever likes us can come aboard." He is being perhaps a trifle disingenuous as at the undistinguished beginnings of the group's career they appeared in as many gay venues as they did straight.

"I'm really proud of our gay following," continued Jason. "We get a load of fan mail from gay men, and I love reading it."

"I just find it very flattering that both sexes seem to fancy us," Robbie added. "Gay audiences like having fun, which we like as well."

The James Deanish actor Luke Perry (who plays angst-ridden Dylan McKay in the television series *Beverly Hills 90210*) was admirably frank in an interview with playwright Kevin Sessums which appeared in *Vanity Fair* (accompanied by strikingly iconographic photographs by Annie Liebovitz). "In any collaborative effort, you have to look past what people represent and what they look like, because you need them for what they can bring to whatever it is you're doing artistically. I don't care if they're gay. I don't care if they're black. I don't care if they're black and gay and a drag queen . . . If they inspire me, those are the people I want around . . . "

Sessums eventually got right to the point. Had Perry "ever experimented sexually with another guy?"

"Flat out, on the record?" Perry responded. "I never have. I've been singularly heterosexual my whole life. So, big deal. Most people have. But to not recognise that there is a homosexual element out there is ridiculous. And *don't* recognise them as some scourge. But see them for what they have to give as people before you define them by their sexuality. Especially in showbusiness: It's fag-o-rama!"

Elsewhere in the thespian community, Christian Slater (*The Name of the Rose*, *Heathers*, *Pump Up the Volume*) has expressed interest in playing a gay role (whilst promoting *Pump Up the Volume*, which includes gay sequences, in *Smash Hits*) and River Pheonix seems set to follow his hustler role in Gus Van Sant's *My Own Private Idaho* in a movie version of Christopher Hampton's 1968 play *Total Eclipse* in which he is slated to play the teenaged gay poet Arthur Rimbaud to John Malkovich's Verlaine.

"Friends have advised me to give my dick a bit of a rest," Adrian Kreye was told by white rapper Marky Mark (brother of New Kids on the Block's Donnie Wahlberg) in the course of an interview which appeared in *Sky*. "They reckon everyone knows I've got one. And I don't keep pulling my trousers down anymore either. Because that's become such a trademark already."

Marky Mark, now an official model for Calvin Klein underwear, is noted for losing his trousers both on and off stage and grabbing his dick by the handful to emphasise it and, presumably, his awareness that that's what his fans – male and female – want to swing from. And, make no mistake, he's completely tuned-in to the fact that he's got

180

gay fans who get turned on by him. "Yo, if you're gay you're in the house, just don't do that shit around me!" he blurts out in an interview in *The Face* "Don't try to fuck me! Bring your sister though, you can watch." So a little exhibitionism for gay males wouldn't worry him . . .

Marky Mark by Marky Mark and Lynn Goldsmith is actually dedicated to his prime attribute: 'I wanna dedicate this book to my dick' he writes on the dedication page, alongside a photograph of himself in typically dick-grabbing pose. 'I wondered how Alma [his mother] would be able to have twice as many girls hanging around outside their home,' photographer Goldsmith writes in her introduction. 'What I didn't know was how many guys would be into Mark as well. I think he attracted both sexes because he came from the streets and has a very strong physical image . . .'

So it appears that for every Axl Rose (Guns`n'Roses) or Shaun Ryder (Happy Mondays) spouting homophobic garbage there is a Take That or East 17 or Marky Mark or Luke Perry who not only acknowledge their gay fans but (*sometimes*) acknowledge homosexual aspects of their own personalities. Whilst we all know that newspapers such as *The Sun* and *The Star* or *The Daily Mail* or *The Daily Express* spew out homophobic stories with a regularity that is utterly and insanely obsessive, the damage they do is most probably to those already diseased. Because by representing positive role models from their readers' peer groups, publications as diverse as *Sky*, *Smash Hits* and *The Face* are encouraging entirely more rational approaches to matters of gaiety and beyond.

GAY TIMES January 1993

NEW KIDS ON THE BLOCK

"Gay writing and publishing has gone mainstream, much as happened with feminist publishing and bookselling, but to a lesser degree," Peter Owen publicist Gary Pulsifer writes in 'Gay Publishing' in *Publishing Now* (Peter Owen). "Gay writers – and gay publishers – have always been around, but it was the publication of Edmund White's novel *A Boy's Own Story* that marked the cross-over point from a writer who was gay to a gay writer heavily hyped and marketed by a mainstream paperback publisher. Now many publishers boast gay authors on their lists, and market them not only to gay and lesbian readers but to a wider audience."

Pulsifer is correct when he states "Gay writers – and gay publishers – have always been around . . . ", but readers had to know what they were looking for and where to look. Those smart young men who sported green carnations in the 1890s would have investigated the lists of new publishers such as The Bodley Head or David Nutt (the latter did Oscar Wilde's *Fairy Tales*); by the turn of the century, interest would have been shown in the list of Greening & Co; in the 1920s and 30s, Phillip Allen or The Hogarth Press might have supplied the books that supplied that special *frisson*; in the 30s, 40s and 50s, readers would have looked towards The Fortune Press (*Fourteen, Fifteen, Sixteen* and all those other 'diaries' by 'a boy', written in fact by the pseudonymous Aubrey Fowkes), John Lehmann (his list included Gore Vidal's *The City and the Pillar*, Tennessee Williams' *The Roman Spring of Mrs Stone* and Denton Welch's *A Last Sheaf*; jackets included designs from Cecil Beaton and John Minton) or W H Allen (publishers of such overdue for reprint gay classics as Rodney Garland's *The Heart in Exile* and Paul Buckland's *Chorus of Witches*).

Some houses remained resolutely heterosexualist, of course: Macmillan is a good "for-instance". And these days Faber & Faber or Chatto & Windus (Armistead

183

Maupin, Patrick Gale, biographies of Daphne Du Maurier, Mary Renault and Genet) generally publish a fair number of titles which once would have been described as of "special interest".

And now there are the exclusively gay publishing houses.

Gay Men's Press was founded in 1979 (first book 1980) by David Fernbach, Aubrey Walter and the late Richard Dipple – initially promoting polemical titles such as Mieli's *Homosexuality and Liberation*, Rosa von Praunheim's *Army of Lovers* and Fernbach's *The Spiral Path*. The books all carried the slogan "Gay Men's Press is an independent publishing project intended to produce books relevant to the male gay movement and to promote the ideas of gay liberation." Design was minimal and unattractive.

With David Rees's *The Milkman's On His way* (1982), with a striking cover design by Francis Michael D'Arcy, and Tom Wakefield's *Mates* (amongst others), GMP moved towards considerably more commercial books which turned the company from polemicist to populist. Today they have a wide and diverse list which ranges from glossy picture books to contemporary fiction (much of it American in origin), classic reprints to valuable studies such as Rictor Norton's *Mother Clap's Molly House*. Although well-established and widely reviewed in the gay press, GMP still struggles for regular and serious attention in the mainstream media. It does seem that – even though specialist gay publishing houses have existed in Britain for over a decade – literary editors are more willing to pay attention to gay writing *coming from a mainstream house* (Adam Mars-Jones and Faber; Edmund White and Chatto & Windus) than they are gay writing *coming from a gay house* (GMP, Trouser Press, Millivres Books).

The more esoteric Brilliance Books was launched at about the same time as GMP – with co-founder Tenebris Light's experimental fiction *Three Rainbows*. Oriented from the beginning towards fiction and reprint fiction (Tennessee Williams' *Moise and the World of Reason*), Brilliance made an early and disastrous mistake by

184

publishing too large an edition of *Title Fight*. Rumour had it that this ill-conceived account of the collapse of *Gay News* had a print run of eight thousand in paperback and two thousand in cloth – but a potential readership of less than a thousand. Brilliance never recovered from this miscalculation – appearing and disappearing as disconcertingly as the Cheshire Cat in *Alice*. One day the smile faded and the company were gone forever ...

Brazen Books, another small (predominantly) fiction list came and went within the blinking of an eye. Third House, founded by novelists David Rees and Peter Robins after both had had problems with GMP, was also small scale – but more enduring. Essentially established to promote their own writing, Third House successfully survived until the end of 1992, when problems arising because of Rees's HIV positive status brought about dissolution of the company. However, Robins, along with the eventual third partner in Third House (novelist Dave Royle) and a new partner (poet Nick Drake) regrouped and Trouser Press rose pheonix-like from the wreckage.

"The aim of trouser press differs very little from that of Third House: the publishing of new gay fiction written in Britain," Robins explains. "This is natural since two of the Trouser Press partners, Dave Royle and myself, were also partners in the old Third House project that flourished from 1987 until last year.

"The decision to found Trouser Press was taken after some consideration. No matter how good any text, a new book now has to be launched into a gay market already awash with texts of gay relevance. To state that we're concentrating mainly on gay readers certainly secures us a constituency, but we must constantly remind ourselves that such readers can only spend their pink pounds once. They too have been hit by the recession.

"Being a small press means that we cannot yet afford large-scale promotion campaigns, nor be over-adventurous in what we publish. But reaction to our first two titles – Dave's *A Controlled Explosion* and my own *Ruined Boys* – has so far been enthusiastic. Yes, reviews have helped, as

185

have window displays. We do suspect, however, that word of mouth remains more important than many suppose."

When Robins points out that "being a small press means that we cannot yet afford large-scale promotion campaigns, nor be over-adventurous in what we publish" he is being at once honest and naive. Not even a company as prominent and as potentially profitable as Gay Men's Press is in a position to undertake large-scale promotions nor be over-adventurous with publishing plans. These are luxuries even the largest companies think twice about. Even so seemingly basic a matter as the dispersal and despatch of review copies has to be seriously considered.

As Millivres Books' solitary functionary, one of my many tasks is to monitor press responses to the books we publish. As a general rule-of thumb we can anticipate some kind of coverage from most sections of the gay press – but attracting the attention of the mainstream press is far more problematic.

A local angle *might* garner local coverage. For example, Sebastian Beaumont's *Heroes Are Hard to Find* is a Brighton-based novel by a Brighton-based author, with a cover graphic of a local landmark by a local artist. That's enough of an angle for the *Brighton Evening Argus* to notice – and led to a highly favourable review. We were also given a generous window display in Read All About It, the best of the town's independent bookshops – which also has a good lesbian and gay section and stock of publications such as *Gay Times* and *Rouge*. But we haven't managed to break through to the "serious" Sunday papers or the likes of *The Times* or *The Independent*.

Our books have received some mainstream coverage – in *The Daily Telegraph*, *The Scotsman* and *The London Magazine* for starters. With the newly published David Evans novel *A Cat in the Tulips*, I completely revised our review list. Out went *Time Out*, which has reviewed only one of the ten titles we have so far published and sent them for consideration. In came *The Daily Express* and *The Daily Mail*, *The Sunday Express*, *The Mail on Sunday* and *The Standard*. *A Cat in the Tulips* is a book of great charm and might just find favour in these less likely papers. It's worth a try.

As a small company, we simply cannot afford to waste books. The entirely London based *Time Out* has proved a waste . . . It's worth looking elsewhere. As Alistair Clarke, Promotions Manager at GMP puts it: "We can't afford to be frivolous with the review copies we send out."

Millivres Books was founded at the very beginning of 1991 and although it is part of the Millivres group of companies (*Gay Times, Him, Vulcan* etc), it operates out of my home and with a tiny team of freelance designers under my direction as the only permanent member of staff. Spurred on by what I see as a deliberate marginalisation of British gay writers and writing (Americans David Leavitt and Edmund White will always get more attention than British Patrick Gale or Tom Wakefield), I determined from the outset that Millivres Books was to be a company specialising in books for gay men (knowing that to aim for an equal opportunities policy with such a small list would be to dilute the impact of the driving philosophy behind my choice of books). I had very deliberately decided to specialise in work which reflected *British* gay experience, feeling that too much of what was published by other houses seemed to reflect a view that it was only *American* experience that counted.

I also hoped to find books that reflected experience that wasn't centred on London, and have so far published books set in York (*On the Edge*), the West Country (*Summer Set*), East Anglia (*Unreal City*), the South Coast (*A Cat in the Tulips*), Brighton (*Heroes Are Hard to Find*) and in Scotland (Graeme Woolaston's *The Learning of Paul O'Neill* to be published in October). If the three E F Benson books we have reissued are to be included, we have also published novels set in Cambridge (*David of Kings*) and Cornwall (*The Inheritor, Ravens' Brood*).

It is evident that there's no shortage of good books "out there" which reflect aspects of British gay life and I already know what Millivres Books will be publishing next year *and* well into 1995 . . .

The newest "kid on the block" so far as gay publishing is

concerned is Cassell, a mainstream house whose Lesbian and Gay studies list debuts this month with Mark E Burke's *Coming Out of the Blue* (gay men, lesbians and bisexuals talk about their lives as police officers) and Edward King's *Safety in Numbers* (gay men and safer sex). Masterminded by commissioning editor Steve Cook and with Liz Gibbs, Christina Ruse and the ubiquitous Peter Tatchell as consultants, Cassell already has around four score titles commissioned and planned for publication over the next three years.

Unlike Gay Men's Press, Millivres Books or Trouser Press, Cassell is a mainstream house – in fact, a small conglomerate which also owns Arms & Armour Press, Blandford Press, Geoffrey Chapman, Victor Gollancz, Mansell Publishing, Mowbray, New Orchard Editions, Studio Vista, Tycooly, Ward Lock and Wisley Handbooks. Between them, the various imprints cross the spectrum from arms and armour to theology, academic to children's books and, in Gollancz, a good all-purpose general publishing list.

"Initially, the idea for Cassell's Lesbian and Gay Studies list was mine," Cook, an activist with groups like OutRage, admits. "We were at a period last spring when we wanted to expand our publishing academic division and so as a publisher in that division I quickly proposed this as the best possible market we could try to enter. I thought it had a real potential for success because I believe that Cassell has that unique combination of both trade and academic operations which meant that we could produce books which would serve an academic need in various subjects whilst those books would also cross-over into a trade market. There was a real need for publishing in this field. No one like *Cassell* had taken the lesbian and gay *general* market seriously – Routeledge, of course, has colonised the gay academic field rather successfully. We identified a gap between what Routeledge are producing in the High Academic field and what the small specialist presses are doing and decided we had the resources to try and prise open the general book trade. This list was actually set up as

Sexual Politics, so it was broader than just Lesbian and Gay Studies – but most of the books we've signed up have come within the Lesbian and Gay Studies remit . . . "

`The Cassell Lesbian and Gay Studies list offers a broad-based platform to lesbian, gay and bisexual writers for the discussion of contemporary issues and for the promotion of new ideas and research,' proclaims a slogan on the inner sleeve of each of the books within Cook's series. And it is in many ways an inevitable list. There's a generous handful of titles which *any* publisher would be pleased to have in their catalogue – Keith Howe's *Broadcasting It*, an encyclopoedia of homosexuality in British broadcasting from 1923 to the present day; Roger Baker's *Drag*, a fully revised and rewritten account of his seminal 1967 history; Richard Smith's *Other Voices*, about gay men and popular music; Rose Collis's biography of Nancy Spain, six years in gestation; Mark Gattis's biography of the film director James Whale. There are titles which will appeal only to specialists and academics (there are at least five "Aids awareness" titles); there are titles which will dip`n'dive between specialist and general readers – books on cinema and theatre, for example; there are a couple of titles which seem destined for the remainder bins even before they are published. There's not exactly "something for everyone", but the potential readership is larger than at first anticipated.

"The other departures which we've made that we hadn't predicted at the start have been opening the list up even more to general categories – for example, we're doing two biographies, so I feel confident that we can take on books like that. Not just because of the Cassell trade and the Cassell academic input into marketing and promoting those books but also because the Victor Gollancz trade are carrying this whole list for us . . . "

Formerly with The Women's Press, Liz Gibbs agrees: "Gollancz recently published a book on J Edgar Hoover and his incredible life. So we can join forces with them to promote particularly biography. The Nancy Spain and the James Whale will benefit greatly from that."

Like (specifically) Millivres Books, Cassell Lesbian and

189

Gay Studies list is keen to avoid "Londoncentricity."

"I lived in Yorkshire for many years, I came out in Yorkshire," Gibbs adds. "I'm very aware of trying to avoid books that suggest London lesbian and gay experience is all there is – certainly in terms of books that we're looking at now but which we haven't signed up yet. Quite a lot of those are from people outside London. I think that by living *in London* you can become so blinkered and imagine that you live in this terribly sympathetic community – which is absolutely crap!"

Between them, Cassell, Millivres Books and Trouser Press, particularly when taken in tandem with such companies as Onlywomen Press and Silver Moon – represent a healthy chunk of lesbian and/or gay led publishing which is being directed by people who share the basic common experience of their potential readers. Something that is not the norm within those mainstream companies who are intent on grabbing a share of the (mythical?) Pink Pound and that may explain why they sometimes get things so disastrously wrong (Faber greedily trying to service both the British *and* American gay communities with two unsuccessful anthologies, one edited by Mars-Jones, *Mae West is Dead*, the other by White, *The Faber Book of Gay Short Fiction*, failing with both because they were neither fish nor fowl nor good read meat).

Recession or no, British gay publishing certainly has muscle to flex and the increase of lists and titles can only be good for both the culture and the individual reader.

GAY TIMES September 1993

REMEMBERING DENIS

My diary reminds me that I first met Denis Lemon in 1972, at the Paddington offices of *Gay News*, the newspaper he had but recently co-founded and of which, by then, he was already sole editor. Denis remained editor – he also became proprietor – until he sold the publication as a result of ill-health in February 1982. During that ten year period, he became perhaps the most prominent gay man in Britain.

Denis had contacted me because I already had some three years' experience in the fledgling world of gay publishing (*Spartacus, Jeremy, Follow-Up*) and he'd correctly assumed that I might have some ideas which would be of interest to him (I had already convinced the novelist Robin Maugham that he should be interviewed for the paper by one of the original collective, David Seligman, to coincide with the publication of his, Maugham's, autobiography, *Escape From the Shadows*). I remember us quickly adjourning to a nearby pub and talking and, more importantly, *laughing*, for some considerable time. It seems entirely appropriate that my earliest memory of him should focus on laughter; Denis and I got on so well together for so many years, in part, at least, because of a great deal of shared laughter. His sense of humour, like mine, was mordant; the blacker the humour, the more it was to his taste.

`Though not easily impressed by people – most especially at first meeting – I quickly warmed to Denis,' I wrote in *Parallel Lives*, a memoir published in 1985. 'I can't remember exactly, but I don't doubt I had a few ideas for the paper which appealed to him. I do remember arranging for *Gay News* to publish Robin Maugham's short story, 'The Boy from Beirut,' in its first Christmas issue. The story was taken from the forthcoming collection, *The Black Tent and Other Stories*, which I'd edited. I convinced Robin to accept a fee of £10.

`My first contribution to the paper appeared the following year and thereafter I became a regular contributor. By early 1976, I was advising Denis on suitable books for review in the newspaper and this led to my being appointed Literary Editor – working on a freelance basis from home as there wasn't space for me in the publication's tiny office.

`Later that same year, I joined the full-time staff of the paper, doubling as Literary Editor and Denis's personal assistant . . . '

Denis and I enjoyed working together, even though the hours were long and the amount of work to be dealt with each day was daunting and exhausting. Almost every evening – after office hours (whatever they were) – we'd decant ourselves to the nearby *Seven Stars* for a few pints and much discussion of future plans.

Invariably I'd be without a pad, so any notes Denis wanted made during the course of our conversation would be scribbled on any available beer mat. The following morning, sense would have to be made of my increasingly drunken scrawl – for Denis liked to have these notes typed and on his desk by the time he arrived in the office. Business and pleasure were inextricably mixed; he worked hard and he played hard – but, unusually, play did not interfere with professional performance.

Often we'd leave the pub and proceed to a restaurant for dinner, sometimes we'd then go on to a club. Often I didn't get home until three in the morning – though generally I was back in the office by ten. There was usually time to sort and sift the mail – before Denis swept into the office demanding tea and the whole process began again.

On one occasion, I had to telephone to explain my absence to the already present Denis.

We'd been particularly drunk the previous evening. 'You remember that cab you helped me into?' I tentatively began.

`Yes,' Denis assented.

`Well, I needed to be sick so I tried to get out . . . The taxi was still moving. My hands are a bit of a mess . . . But I'll be in later.'

`Not too late, I hope,' Denis commented drily. The humour of others is always hard to define: Denis's drollery could easily be mistaken for something else.

It was in 1976 that Denis received two unsolicited poems from James Kirkup – one concerned the discovery by Robinson Crusoe of the corpse of Friday on the island foreshore and his subsequent sodomising of it, and the other, 'The love that dares to speak its name', was eventually published in *Gay News* 96 in June of that year. This 'dealt with a gay man's conversion to Christianity and metaphorically attributed homosexual acts to Jesus Christ', as Denis wrote in an article published in *Gay Times* in July 1992. 'Shocking, eccentric, graphically outspoken (and probably not a great work of literature), the poem to me – and I hope to those who bothered to read it – would say something meaningful, at the very least to be thought provoking.

`For too long gay men and women had suffered from the homophobic hostility of large sections of the religious establishments. By contrast, I thought the message and intention of the poem was to celebrate the absolute universality of God's love, even if in doing so Professor Kirkup used sexual explicitness in his imagery.

Not everyone saw the poem in the same light. When it was brought to her attention by an outraged reader, Mrs Mary Whitehouse initiated a prosecution for blasphemous libel against *Gay News* and Denis Lemon. John Mortimer acted for the defence in the trial which opened at the Old Bailey on 4th July 1977. Judge Alan King-Hamilton refused to allow expert testimony from witnesses who would have spoken of the literary, sociological and even theological merits of the work – though Margaret Drabble and Bernard Levin were allowed to appear as 'character' witnesses with regard to the content of the paper. The trial concluded with Gay News Ltd being fined £1000 and ordered to pay its own costs and Denis being fined £500 and given a nine month prison sentence, suspended for eighteen months. Hearings at the Court of Appeal (which quashed the prison sentence) and the House of Lords were ineffective. The verdict stood.

But the prosecution and trial, the first of its kind since

1922, attracted media attention around the world and gained for *Gay News* more valuable publicity than it could ever have generated for itself. The blasphemy trial brought to the attention to hundreds – if not thousands – of isolated gay men and lesbians the existence of a gay press. Inadvertently, Mrs Whitehouse had done those she wished to do down a genuine service. And Denis found himself a celebrity and in demand as a public speaker and a private personality. His life was changed forever and even as recently as a few weeks before his death, broadcasters were trying to contact him with regards his appearing on yet another programme about blasphemy.

Born in Bradford-on-Avon in Wiltshire in 1945, Denis grew up in Herne Bay and Whitstable and was educated at the Simon Langton School in Canterbury. Moving to London, he worked in accountancy and later in a record shop in south London – music was an obsession. The evolving Gay Liberation Front pulled him in the direction of sexual politics and the idea for *Gay News* was first mooted in 1971. The first issue – run by a short-lived collective – appeared in June 1972. Denis became editor in August, remaining in that position until he sold the paper ten years later. *Gay News* did not long survive his departure.

Although he had written for *Gay News* and more recently contributed to *Gay Times* (book reviews and, notably, his own account of the blasphemy prosecution and trial), Denis was not a journalist and his vital contribution to gay publishing was as a far-sighted entrepreneur who was hard nosed enough to get a gay newspaper successfully combining politics and entertainment up-and-running and keep it going in the face of hostility.

Denis was perhaps the most exacting, most demanding editor I ever wrote for. His meticulousness when editing copy was positively nineteenth century – he would telephone a writer to consult them about the placing of a comma, the use of the archaic 'k' at the end of 'gothick', the accuracy of detail and fact. He cared passionately. That kind of attention and concern for copy simply doesn't exist today – be it in the mainstream or in the more specialist byways of publishing. "How do you spell 'lettuce'?" he asked me as he went through the restaurant column I was by then contributing.

As I patently couldn't spell the bloody word, I couldn't locate it in the dictionary. Denis corrected my spelling – but I thought I might have to write the word out a hundred times just to ensure I knew how to spell it in future. My Christmas present in 1979 was the dictionary in which I again looked up the spelling of 'lettuce' as I drafted this memoir.

But Denis was considerably more than just an editor for whom I worked. We socialised in London, New York – more latterly in Brighton and Exeter. Denis met large numbers of my friends – Robin Maugham wondered whether they had a common ancestor in the Victorian humourist and editor of *Punch*, Mark Lemon. Denis was one of the guests at the Christmas I hosted for family and friends in 1976 and my father and mother were thrilled to see 'that nice young man' on television the following summer – when Denis was appearing at the Old Bailey on that charge of blasphemous libel.

Denis Lemon was a man of immense charm, caustic wit, shining intelligence and great entrepreneurial skill. His range of artistic, cultural and political interests ensured that the time spent in his company was invigorating – even sometimes intellectually and/or physically exhausting. Even after illness had taken hold, Denis showed himself far more capable of keeping going on our infrequent meetings than I was myself. He could run a fit person ragged. And he made friends and enemies in about equal measure – he didn't suffer fools gladly and suffered only pin-pricks from those who were jealous; he greatly respected competence, excellence, hard-work, endeavour. He was – on the whole – a fair man.

With *Gay News* behind him, Denis became a restaurateur – first in London, more latterly in Exeter, at the Arts Centre, after he'd retreated to that city in an attempt to regain the anonymity he had lost as a result of publishing the poem that Kirkup has long since dishonourably disowned. He

195

had suffered from Aids-related illness for several years, and ill-health caused him to become increasingly reclusive, but with a hold on life the tenacity of which amazed his friends.

When Derek Jarman died in February, Denis telephoned me. He was distressed by the end of someone whom he had admired more than I. He must have known that his own physical resources were sadly depleted – but discussed driving to Brighton for a visit. Could my household cope? Of course, I said – but didn't, in truth, believe he would ever make that journey, and nor did he.

'I was close to the edge last week,' Denis told me on April 9th. 'Time is running out.' My diary entry for that date concludes, 'though he's said that before . . .'

Denis's courage in the face of a particularly cruel illness, which robbed him of his mobility while leaving his mind alert, was magnificent. And to the end he had the support of his partner, Nick Purshouse, and the companionship of his many, beloved cats. My world is emptier without him – he was a great original, to be remembered with love and pride.

GAY TIMES September 1994

AFTERWORD

A week is a long time in publishing. And twenty-five years is 1300 long times. I was one year old when the first essay in this collection was published. Male homosexuality had not long been decriminalised, and the gay press and a recognisable gay scene were both in their infancy. Just like me. All of us have done quite a bit of growing up since then.

Peter Burton has spent half his life working for the gay press. *Amongst the Aliens* may be subtitled 'Some aspects of a gay life' but this book reveals a great deal about all gay men's lives. We've come a long way in the last quarter of a century. And when I say "we" I mean anyone under twenty-five as well. Whatever our age, we share the same past. *Amongst the Aliens* will be of interest to anyone who recognises that in uncovering the past we learn how to move forward.

Some of Peter Burton's essays here deal with abiding passions of his: books, food and pretty young men in pop groups. Others cover what now appear to be perennial gay male concerns; jealousy, living together, queerbashing, homophobia and growing old. However the two most moving pieces are about something that no one foresaw back in 1970, where Peter remembers two close friends lost to Aids, Ian McGee and Denis Lemon.

Whether he's smashing tired gay myths like the "pink pound" or revealing a sneaking admiration for Ronnie Kray, Burton's writing never fails to be provocative and lively. He has also always shown an admirable readiness to tackle objects others would rather ignore; be it the complex interaction between class, age, race and homosexuality, or the "touchy" topics of cottaging, cruising and promiscuity. Peter quite rightly takes these last three things as gay blessings not blights. And if a horse ever got his hooves on a copy of this book he'd be jolly frightened indeed. Which is exactly how it should be.

In these pages you can also discover (or remember) the clothes we once wore, the haircuts we had, the words we used, the clubs we favoured, the records we loved and the pin ups we put on our walls. Unlike most books which claim to be "gay histories" *Amongst the Aliens* builds a picture of how we really used to live.

Richard Smith